Praise for *Uncompromising*

"Modern culture has low expectations for girls. It expects them to be consumed with jealousy and insecurity—obsessed with their outward appearance. It doesn't expect them to attain any level of character beneath the surface. Hannah Farver is on a mission to change that. Even more exciting, she comes from the ranks of the young women she is reaching. Her voice is wise and witty—but also relevant. Girls today need a clear vision of biblical, beautiful womanhood. Hannah provides just that."

—ALEX AND BRETT HARRIS, bestselling authors of
Do Hard Things and *Start Here*

"With insight, wit, and grace, Farver discusses some popular causes that seek to captivate the heart of today's young woman. May her call to be uncompromising stir an entire generation to set aside the lesser in order to embrace the greatest Cause of all!"

—MARY A. KASSIAN, speaker, author of *Girls Gone Wise*,
and professor at Southern Seminary

"I've read plenty of outstanding books on the subject of bold, faithful femininity—but all were geared toward adult women. With *Uncompromising*, Hannah Farver supplies a well-written, engaging book that is a hearty embrace of all God intends for female Christ-followers who are entering their adult years. But unlike many other materials for young adults, this book is not patronizing or shallow. Rather, it sets a high bar for the passions and hopes that young women have—and points readers to the Cause that is worth it all."

—CAROLYN MCCULLEY, author of *Radical Womanhood*
and *Did I Kiss Marriage Goodbye?*

"*Uncompromising* should be a must-read book for every young girl! Hannah's story not only encourages, but challenges. She has such a profound ability of putting into words what all young girls go through at some point in their life."

—SHANNON STEWART RATLIFF, model and runner-up on
America's Next Top Model

"This is the book I wanted to write when I was Hannah's age. Now I'm reaching out to twentysomethings, and I'm looking back wondering who's going to affect today's teen AS a teen. Hannah Farver is it. She is that girl. She's no longer hiding or allowing the world to take any more young women as prisoners. Hooray! I hope every teen or mother of teens will pick up a copy. The future is now!"

—RENEE JOHNSON, author of *Faithbook of Jesus*

"Young women today face more challenges than previous generations, and this book points out timeless truths from God's Word on where they can find their *true* worth."

—HEATHER ARNEL PAULSEN, author of *Emotional Purity*

"Women of all ages should read this book, which covers many of the topics we all struggle with, even as Christians: beauty, relationships, modesty, and purity. Farver's fun, fresh, and compassionate take on the truth that beauty is not what people see on the outside, but who God made us on the inside."

—ANN-MARGRET HOVSEPIAN, author of *The One Year Designer Genes Devotional*

"In this book, Hannah takes a stand for girlhood God's way. It's a battle cry for young women everywhere who want to live lives patterned after God's Word. Throughout this book Hannah will inspire you to apply the language of God's Word to every corner of your life and learn to live without compromise. If you're willing to fight back against the lies of the culture consider this book standard issue armor."

—ERIN DAVIS, author of *Graffiti: Learning to See the Art in Ourselves*

Uncompromising

A Heart Claimed
by a Radical Love

HANNAH FARVER

MOODY PUBLISHERS

CHICAGO

Edited by Annette LaPlaca Interior design: Ragont Design
Cover design: Maralynn Rochat Cover photos: Swirl and Texture: iStockphoto
Author photo: Michaella Elliott

Library of Congress Cataloging-in-Publication Data

Farver, Hannah.
    Uncompromising : a heart claimed by a radical love / Hannah Farver.
    p. cm.
    Includes bibliographical references (p.   ).
    ISBN 978-0-8024-1167-9
    1. Young women—Religious life. 2. Love—Religious aspects—Christianity.
I. Title.
BV4551.3.F38 2011
248.8'33—dc22

                                                    2011002847

We hope you enjoy this book from Moody Publishers. Our goal is to provide high-quality, thought-provoking books and products that connect truth to your real needs and challenges. For more information on other books and products written and produced from a biblical perspective, go to www.moodypublishers.com or write to:

Moody Publishers
820 N. LaSalle Boulevard
Chicago, IL 60610

1 3 5 7 9 10 8 6 4 2

Printed in the United States of America

To Grace and Miriam

Contents

Foreword

by Brett Harris

I first met Hannah Farver in 2007 when she helped host a teen conference my brother Alex and I were holding in Dallas. We were so impressed we asked her again the following year. By that time she was already authoring an outstanding blog for young women called Beauty from the Heart (www.beautyfromtheheart.org) and was getting ready to launch her own series of conferences.

A year later Hannah e-mailed us about a book she was writing and asked us to look over the manuscript. Well aware of her exceptional character and competence, we gladly agreed—and were thrilled by what we read. When she asked us to consider writing the foreword, we didn't have to think twice.

Since then, Hannah has joined us at Patrick Henry College where we've had the opportunity to attend classes together, enjoy British movie nights (with tea), and build a statue of Cary Grant out of snow (her idea). Alex and I have watched her practice what she preaches day in and day out, amidst the pressures of exams and the drama of college life. Even though we are a few years older, we have personally benefited from the "big sister" wisdom God has given her.

Simply put: Hannah Farver is the real deal, a young woman of conviction, compassion, and courage. Through her words and her example she is provoking young women to raise their sights and fix their gaze on the only Cause and the only Love worth pursuing. She is a fresh and compelling voice straight from the ranks of her peers. Her passion for God, and for her generation, flows through every chapter and bleeds through every page.

One of the things Alex and I love about *Uncompromising* is that Hannah is not a grown-up trying to sound like a girl. She is a girl wrestling with grown-up things like purity, modesty, and what it means to be a woman. Her challenge to our generation is firmly rooted in her own humble (and often humorous) search for something greater than the trinkets and trappings of this world. These dispatches from a girl-in-progress carry a gut-level honesty—the emotions are fresh; the excitement is real; the journey has begun.

As Hannah writes, "Take this book as the collected scribblings of someone who has met—and is still learning to adopt (or be adopted by)—the Cause. It's a work in progress, but maybe my notes will help you compile your own."

If you accept Hannah's invitation to come face-to-face with Jesus Christ, you will never be the same again, and you will never regret it. What she describes as "scribblings" are nothing less than a soul-shattering tribute to the greatest Cause that ever was or ever will be.

—BRETT HARRIS

Brett Harris (along with his twin brother, Alex) founded TheRebelution.com and authored the bestselling books *Do Hard Things: A Teenage Rebellion Against Low Expectations* and *Start Here: Doing Hard Things Right Where You Are.*

She made a conscious choice to trust in God, to take His word as truth, to see opportunity and to wear His praises publicly on her lips . . . and she did not find Him disappointing.

—ANDREE SEU

The Truth
about Causes
(An Intro You Shouldn't Skip)

A poet named Maud Kelly once wrote of reaching "the point I always knew would come, when I was at once too old and far too young, how I knew, really knew for the first time that there's a wildness in us."

I think I know what she was talking about.

Right now, I'm sipping a mug of black coffee. Not the tastiest thing in the world (the froufrou stuff tastes best), but it wakes me up. I need it today.

My problem is, I have a hard time writing unless my heart is exploding. Okay, maybe not exploding but feeling intensely. This becomes a bit of a hassle, because 90 percent of the time I'm not there.

My guess is that the same is true of you. Do you have a few things that you do just because you love them? Do they make you feel awake, as if today's your first day and you're sensing everything afresh? Maybe you feel energized when you're writing music. Maybe you sense the passion when you run or swim or speak your mind. Maybe you get worked up when you talk politics. Whatever your "thing" is, that passion helps keep you going. Sometimes you have to pump yourself full of coffee to trick your body into imitating that passion, but you can't replace the real thing. That passion is what makes you, you.

We're meant to have a cause. There's a reason for the "wildness in us."

You and I are most alive when we are passionate about something. Our brains speed up. We become more sensitive to our surroundings. Our emotions take an exit from "average," and we start to feel intensely. I think there's a meaning behind this phenomenon.

We were hardwired for passion.

Not just momentary emotional highs.

Not short-lived bursts of inspiration.

You and I were created to have overall purpose etched into our lives. That purpose becomes a passion that—whether we always feel it or not—helps to guide our decisions and defines the way we live.

We're meant to have a cause—a mission. There's a reason for the "wildness in us."

Though school, relationship drama, worries, and the

general buzz of life can steal our attention away—we're meant for more. Our wildness was created on purpose, an echo of our Creator. Call it a longing for forever in a world of what's temporary; call it a cry to the heavens for some unbroken place to stand. We were created for God. While we may funnel our passion into other things—like school, friends, status, success, popularity, and daily worries—we were originally designed to funnel our passion into giving God glory.

We were made for more than a list of causes. We were made for One.

Some people who recognized their particular wildness allowed their lives to be changed, singlemindedly pouring all their passion into that single purpose. One young mother in ancient Africa threw herself so completely into the Cause that when the emperor himself tried to make her give it up, she chose imprisonment instead. Time after time, Perpetua was commanded to give up the Cause. She refused, even as she faced the beasts in the arena that would take her life. And you know what? To the death, she knew she'd chosen well. The Cause was more valuable than life.

One Scottish woman became so passionate about the Cause that she determined to share it with others. Amy Carmichael left home and traveled to India, where she worked to rescue orphan girls from sex slavery, long before sex trafficking became a widely publicized issue. She did not return to her homeland, but poured out her years helping children the world had forgotten. She's buried in India, where her adoptive children built a birdbath over her grave, to remember the beauty of her life.

It was the love of the Cause that led a man to say, after spending night after night chained in a Chinese prison simply for preaching the gospel, "I will preach until I die."[1]

Like heroes and history-changers throughout time, you know you were made for something beyond yourself. If you've ever felt afraid of that ultimate purpose, don't be. It's wooing you. You've felt it sneak up on you, taking a giant spoon and stirring up your soul, calling you in a voice that seeps into your bones and makes itself unforgettable. The ultimate Cause is calling you.

If we come face-to-face with the Cause, we will never be the people we were before.

Too often, we confuse the Cause with other causes with small c's. I've mistaken it tons of times, pursuing wild goose chases such as beauty, acceptance, and even "respectable causes" like other people's esteem or love. (Who doesn't want to feel respected and cherished?) But those chases have left me empty-handed, feeling silly and used.

This book is about the big Cause and the little causes

that get in the way, how the Cause affects our lives, and how there's enough room and mission and purpose and passion in the Cause to go around.

Now, I realize this is a book and we're not technically spending time together. I want to clarify that right off. I always feel a little creeped out when I read a book where the author pretends she knows me and that I'm her best friend. I'll be up front and say, "I don't know you at all, (though I'd be thrilled to meet you sometime)."

If we ever do meet, I can't promise you'll like me. I have an opinion on almost everything, and if the other person in conversation is very quiet, I feel the need to fill up the air with the sound of my own voice. I jump into decisions impetuously. I like overproduced, auto-tuned pop music. Clearly, I'm a very imperfect person.

So please don't take this book as me preaching at you. If I do come across as preachy, just shake your head. Remember, I'm that girl with problems, and you're a girl with problems too, and maybe if we're honest truth-seekers who speak in enough love, we'll come out of this feeling a little better and a little wiser.

Scratch that. I can't promise we'll feel "a little better and a little wiser"—and I'm not even sure that's a good goal to have. Who wants only "a little" of anything good? Frankly, I'm not sure I can even deliver that.

Here's the only thing I can say: *If you and I come face-to-face with the Cause, I guarantee we will never be the people we were before.* We will cease to revolve around the sun as our lives find a new, blazing center. Our search for a purpose to define our existence will end. We will not run out of questions, but we will, at last, find the Answer to all things.

Take this book as the collected scribblings of someone who has met—and is still learning to adopt (or be adopted by)—the Cause. It's a work in progress, but maybe my notes will help you compile your own.

Now, so many years

later, I can see the fear beginning to take shape in little girls' eyes. I see their furtive glances at the magazines, the gleam of something like lust that shines in their eyes as they feed on the glossy pages. I see them stand behind a beautiful woman and trace the lines of her figure with their eyes, holding their crossed arms over their own bodies. I see them searching through advertisements for cologne, shampoo, dental bleach, lipstick . . . hoping to find their own faces.

—BETHANY PIERCE, painter and novelist

One Way
to Get Sick

I had never put on eyeliner before—at least, not correctly. I didn't even own any. Digging through Mom's bathroom cabinet, I found an eyeliner pencil and decided to give it a shot. Anything was worth trying after what I'd just done to my face. A glance at the clock told me I still had some time.

For weeks, I had been planning a day trip to a theme park with some friends. I liked roller coasters, and I liked my friends. That wasn't the problem. The mounting problem was the beauty procedure I had attempted on myself the night before the theme park trip.

With one fateful look in the mirror, I had decided my eyebrows needed a change. Gazing from a razor to my eyebrows, an idea began to take shape. Picking up the razor, I held it to my face.

If you guessed I shaved my eyebrow, you're right. The night before our long-awaited theme park day, I shaved off almost exactly half of my left eyebrow. If someone had taken a giant rubber eraser and wiped off half my face, I couldn't have felt more bald.

Yet this was only the beginning. I also faced the impossible challenge of trying to look normal until my eyebrow grew back. I tilted my head lopsidedly. There. If only no one would notice I was walking around as though my neck were broken sideways, maybe I could give the illusion that my eyebrows were even . . . or not.

It wasn't going to work.

My second impossible challenge was hiding my lack of eyebrow from Mom, who, I was certain, would rebuke me for my vanity.

The next morning unfolded like a miracle. In the frenzy of packing peanut butter and jelly sandwiches, sunscreen, and piling my younger siblings in the car, Mom didn't even notice.

The theme park ended up not being so bad either. My friends didn't seem to realize that my eyebrows were a little more painted-looking than usual.

Then the storm hit.

Rain, lightning, thunder, hail—the whole shebang pounded the theme park. Crowded beneath an awning, we all waited out the storm, watching as puddles the size of goldfish ponds formed around our ankles.

It was then that I began to receive funny looks. My conscience began to throb (if that's possible), and if ever I felt guilty for being too vain, it was then.

Mom suddenly stared. "There's something on your face."

I wiped my face with my hand and noticed black streaks. Uh-oh. I'd forgotten to check if the eyeliner was waterproof. Mom stared some more. Then it came.

"Hannah, is that black stuff makeup?"

"Uh . . . well . . . yeah . . . sorta . . . "

Later, when she had time to inspect my stub of a brow, Mom learned the whole story. You can imagine that dialogue.

I'd like to say I learned a deep lesson that day that changed my life forever. But if I learned a lesson at all, it was only that if you have something to hide, make sure the eyeliner is waterproof!

In the mirror I saw how God had made me to look and I hated what He'd done.

My vanity makes for a pretty funny story now. I've been teased about it plenty of times. But after the eyebrow-meets-razor incident, I didn't get any smarter. Instead I grew more and more focused on looking better and finding acceptance by changing my appearance. It stopped being funny at all. Beauty became one of the causes that took over my mind and ambitions. And by this pursuit of outward beauty, I was left disappointed.

God loved me. I had known this for as long as I could remember. I was taught in church and at home by my parents that He created me and loved me as I was. But deception sneaked in as I reached young adulthood, until every time I looked in the mirror, all I saw was ugliness. One thing I've learned since then: It doesn't ever really matter what you look like, so long as you're convinced that you are lacking, you'll never be content. This obsession can distort your view of everything. So no matter how I looked that day, in the mirror I saw how God had made me to look and I hated what He'd done. My nose was too big, my lips too small, and—most importantly—my waistline too large. It called for drastic measures.

When mealtime came, I was "no longer hungry." I skipped countless meals. At dinnertime with family around the table, I tried to eat tiny portions. I began comparing myself to movie stars, models in magazines, and skinny people I knew to find further motivation to stop eating.

For the most part, I managed to hide my new eating habits (or not-eating habits) from my mom. When she raised her eyebrows, I would say, "It's funny. I don't know why, but I've just lost my appetite lately. I guess it's hormonal or something."

Often I'd give in to temptation and make cookies or something chocolaty to make myself feel better. Afterward, I'd feel guilty and promise not to eat anything else all day, but thanks to my inconsistency, I didn't lose much weight and probably couldn't be labeled as anorexic or bulimic. But my mind—it had gotten seriously sick. I had thoughts of suicide, depression. You know the pattern: I had no place to rest my hope, and I got lost trying to find that resting place.

Now, don't get your hopes up for a dramatic conclusion. Mine is not a particularly exciting story. Even though my heart did eventually change, I still fight with these beauty-thoughts to some degree. On worse days, I don't even fight. I let them carve inches off my sense of worth until something shakes me awake and reminds me it isn't right, this obsession.

At first, right after the-skipping-meals-calorie-counting-stuff happened, I was embarrassed to tell anyone. My parents had a hard time believing the story. They said they had known I was struggling, but I'd succeeded in hiding the extent of my obsession with weight loss from them. So it's weird to share this story here, except I have a feeling you might be able to relate.

Studies indicate that seven million American women have an eating disorder, and 95 percent of those who have eating disorders are between the ages of twelve and twenty-five.[1] These may seem like dry numbers. Rather than shoving the statistics into some obscure corner of our minds where we'll never think of them again, let's try to realize that each number represents a sister, neighbor, or best friend—young women threatened by a cause that consumes them. Since you're a thinking person and probably won't just take what I say for granted, I want to prove to you how painful it can be to pursue short-lived causes like outward beauty. Let's try to understand these numbers.

VISITING THE MALL

Suppose it's your friend's birthday. She's invited you to browse the mall with her in honor of the occasion. You've just completed some hard-core shopping, and now you're parched. After treating yourself to a _____ milkshake (this is a fantasy, so pick your favorite flavor), you both rest your legs on a nearby bench.

A number of shoppers stroll by. You barely finish the whipped cream topping before ten teenage girls have passed. Some are preppy, some are emo, but they all have something in common. What you can't see from the outside is that five out of those ten girls think their weight is "too high." Half of them personally know someone who has an eating disorder. Out of the thirteen-year-old girls who have passed, 80 percent have tried dieting.[2]

Your straw is making that slurping noise, signaling that your milkshake is nearly finished. By this point, one hundred young women have walked by your bench. (So it's a really crowded mall.) Although you've barely noticed them, each girl has a different life story; each could probably share personal struggles before the mirror. Of the one hundred girls, seven will return home to vomit. They hope that keeping their stomachs shrunken and hungry will help them stay or become thin.[3] The other shoppers could easily sympathize because, out of those one hundred girls, more than half have attempted to lose weight.[4]

Hurting and sometimes permanently harming themselves,

girls imagine once they achieve the super (thin) model image, their problems will end. Chasing desperately after this goal, they miss an important truth: Barbie is made of plastic.

HOW?

Beauty is one of the most common struggles among the girls I know. It's often private, and we want to laugh it off. Nobody wants to admit to being shallow. People might think we're stupid, or—worse—they might see our true frailty—so we pretend it's no big deal. But the truth is, if any cause promises us enough, we'll chase it. Beauty included.

What was the point of that little "visit to the mall" exercise? Well, one of the big reasons girls are obsessed with beauty is that they want to be unique. They want to be noticed. They want to turn heads (specifically a head belonging to an oh-so-single hunk), but in reality when girls and women starve to be beautiful, they only start looking like everybody else.

I grew up in a household where my parents tried to de-emphasize beauty as much as possible. I wasn't allowed to wear makeup as a child. In home videos, it's clear that I was the kid who wanted to wear the ratty overalls with one broken strap. How do normal little girls like me get so sick in the head?

We're brainwashed. When a lie is repeated long

enough, it blends into the scenery until we stop challenging it. Like a broken window or a room that hasn't been cleaned for months, our surroundings become normal. We forget that this lie has not always existed and we have not always believed it.

We could blame Barbie, cruel, selfish advertisers, and plastic surgeons. You're probably expecting me to blame them, too—and I do. But the people primarily deserving the blame are you and me. Why do I say this? Because while advertisers certainly supply us with lies, training our subconscious minds to think that beauty is being 5'9", 110 pounds, and having full lips—we're the ones who actually fall for them. We're the ones who care.

Now, beauty is just one example of a cause we foolishly chase. It's certainly not the only cause that can distract us, and it's not the only one worth writing about. But the unique thing about the beauty cause is how *clearly* it is a counterfeit.

WHAT BEAUTY HAS
TO DO WITH CAUSES

All little causes are counterfeits of the one Cause that will give us real satisfaction. With beauty, the counterfeit factor is just a little more obvious.

We think beauty will buy us love. If you don't believe me, just think, would beauty be important if we didn't also want the admiration that supposedly follows being beautiful? Have you ever found yourself dressing to attract a guy or applying heavy makeup just to be noticed? Then you know what I'm trying to say. We think beauty equals love, and love is a cause all of us want to get behind.

Guys like girls, especially the pretty ones. Of course, the ultimate authority on all things female—chick flicks—affirm this. We also witness this firsthand at the mall, school, or church, where the young man's arm is looped securely around the pretty blonde's shoulders.

Not that all those who want beauty necessarily want a boyfriend, but the root problem is still the same. Whether love is found from the approval of friends, from the acceptance of the world, or from ourselves, the search for beauty often finds its source here.

We may be disgusted with ourselves for caring so deeply for what others think. Or we may be accustomed to the insecurity. Either way, we've got a mess on our hands, because we've confused love with getting attention. We've turned beauty into some kind of cheap replacement for real love and satisfaction, so much so that we don't know what love is anymore. And that's a huge, huge problem.

But if we reject the substitutes, where can love be found? To find it, we'll need to remember what it is first.

The love for equals is a human thing—of friend for friend, brother for brother. It is to love what is loving and lovely. The world smiles. The love for the less fortunate is a beautiful thing—the love for those who suffer . . . This is compassion, and it touches the heart of the world. The love for the more fortunate is a rare thing— to love those who succeed where we fail, to rejoice without envy with those who rejoice, the love of the poor for the rich . . . The world is always bewildered by its saints. And then there is the love for the enemy— love for the one who does not love you but mocks, threatens and inflicts pain. The tortured's love for the torturer. This is God's love. It conquers the world.

—FREDERICK BUECHNER,
The Magnificent Defeat

CHAPTER 2

On Love
and Imitations

I'm going to tell you a story. First, I'm going to say right away that I will not do it justice. Second, just so you know, this story is true—ish.

Alexis felt the van slam on its brakes and skid to a halt. Horns blared behind her. She flew forward, her cheek hitting the side door, bruising.

She didn't care.

There was an empty parking lot up the street, the driver said. They could wait there. The man in the passenger's seat mumbled an assent. She could hear him on the phone. He repeated the location. He named a meeting time.

The light must've changed. Full speed ahead.

The van jostled like a Land Rover over the bumps. Alexis tried to take note of everything the man said, trying to visualize where she was, like kidnapping victims in the movies did. If she could figure out where she was, she might guess where they were taking her . . .

But what would that matter, if no one was looking for her? She hadn't heard anything about a ransom. And if one was offered, who would even pay?

Alexis huddled in the dark. There was that saltiness again on her tongue. Blood. She wished she could spit it out, but the duct tape around her mouth wouldn't let her. She swallowed.

She tried wrenching her wrists free, but they were tied. So were her ankles—and her knees.

All she could do was lie there, listening: the hum of trucks speeding on the overpass, the faint whine of a siren, and the thick vibrations of a booming stereo down the street.

The street sounds echoed memories of her former home, always accompanied by fear. Her father shouting. Her mom screaming. The look on her brother's swollen face—pride and bravery—while he lied and said he'd only tripped on the stairs. The day she caught him dealing on the street. The men who came by the house—men whose money put food on the table and whose touch made Alexis feel like a body that forgot it encased a soul.

On the day of her high school graduation, she'd packed up and moved from her neighborhood—anything to escape that world.

When she met David, Alexis thought he would act as a transfusion, a brand-new start in a brand-new life as his wife.

Alexis knew she was undeserving. She was only averagely intelligent, rarely funny, and certainly missed the mark where beauty was concerned. He could've married anybody, but David chose her, Alexis, the girl whose idea of a healthy marriage came from watching Disney movies.

Yet no matter how hard she had fought and kicked and clawed for a new beginning, the dirt of her past ran in her veins. It seemed to be who she was, part of her blood. She felt guilty, living in a perfect house, being cherished by the kindest man on earth. She remained guilty and restless.

Before long, time added glitter to the past. She convinced herself that those dark early years weren't really so bad. Sure, there were shootings and drug deals, but Alexis wasn't some delicate flower. She wondered if, after all, that world was where she belonged.

Only the week before she had tried to go back. She reclaimed old contacts, starting up the old business. But the old contacts had changed. The streets had grown harsher, if that were possible. Her brother was no longer around.

And now she was being shipped off against her will, like a slave. At last, she understood. These past few days of crazily trying to recapture her old life wasn't like she had imagined. It tasted less like an adventure and more like dying from the inside out.

There was no question in Alexis's mind that this was the end. No human being had that much mercy—not even David. He would never take her back.

She tried not to cry. The tears were suffocating. With duct tape on her mouth, she found it hard to breathe, but she couldn't stop the tears. As the hours passed, she lost consciousness.

"What is love?" is a question
that has stumped philosophers
and poets for centuries.

As I said, Alexis's story is true, but if I tell you the ending, you might not believe me. You'll probably think I'm quoting the story line of a movie. I wouldn't blame you either, because people just don't seem to love each other in a self-denying way in real life.

Here's how it ended:

The van door slid open. Alexis blinked as the sunlight hit her face. She hadn't felt such light in days and could hardly see anything in the brightness.

Her heart thudded. Was this the end? What would they do to her now? What more could they do? There was so little of her left undamaged! Inside her head, she prayed God would do her one last favor and let her die right there. She closed her eyes, waiting for death.

Instead, she felt gentle hands peel the duct tape from her mouth. She winced, but had no voice left for screaming. Eyes suddenly wide-open, she thought for a second she was seeing a mirage. It was David. He sawed at the tape around her wrists, then her knees, then her ankles.

"We need to get out of here," he whispered to her.

Alexis managed to nod. She knew she couldn't speak. She hadn't had water in many hours. She hoped he could guess her question, that he could see her sorrow.

"Don't worry," he said. "I bought you back."

Oh, where, oh, where had her words gone? "I'm . . . sorry," she barely got the words out. It was all she could say. For David, it was enough.

David had heard of his wife's captivity. Of course he realized that she was the one who had put herself in danger—that she had returned to a life of prostitution and turned her back on his love and commitment. In fact, word of his wife's prostitution brought shame to him and his entire family and threatened all he'd worked for in his career. The cheating he knew about all too well.

Rather than simply call slavery the "consequences" of her decision, David went after her. He hunted down Alexis's captors. He demanded to buy her back and paid for her freedom from his own bank account. Even though she'd played with his emotions and humiliated him by making him look like a fool, he bought back her life and freedom. Alexis then became more David's wife than she ever had been before, because now she understood that his love was all she wanted.

STIRRED, BUT NEVER SHAKEN

"What is love?" is a question that has stumped philosophers and poets for centuries. For many of us, "love" automatically triggers thoughts of pink hearts, flowers, chocolate, naked baby angels, and *You've Got Mail*. (Oh? You don't think of naked baby angels? Actually, me neither.)

Believe it or not, the dictionary's definition is just as shallow. Love is defined as ". . . a deep . . . feeling of affection . . . such as that arising from kinship, recognition of attractive qualities, or a sense of underlying oneness. A feeling of intense desire and attraction toward a person with whom one is disposed to make a pair."[1]

Does that sound strange to you? If you notice, that definition is filled with words describing love as a "feeling" or a "desire." According to the dictionary, love is based on our emotions toward a person—or how well we are treated. "Love" by this definition is a bratty two-year old, attention-demanding and happy only so long as he receives an unlimited supply of what it wants. If the kid does not get toys and candy—well, you may want to leave the room.

This is the kind of love we imagine is drawn only by physical beauty. It's the "love" you can get with toned legs and tight shirts, the kind of "love" that leaves you with the memory of a one-night stand and an empty heart.

Feelings fade. Eventually something goes against our expectations. We don't get what we want, and our emotions head for the rocks, dragging our last "lovey feelings" with them. But should love be so unstable, begging for attention, based on our emotions? Is love so wimpy? Or perhaps we've been missing real love altogether.

When I was a girl, a visit to my grandparents' house meant witnessing the unpleasant reality of my grandfather's Alzheimer's disease. Upon our arrival at their home, my grandfather would reach out his arms to me for an embrace, welcoming his "darling." It wasn't until I was older that I realized he said "darling" because he couldn't remember my name.

My grandfather was once famous for his lively stories about living in Nigeria, Ghana, Palau, and South Korea, but most of his personality was lost when time ate his memories. All that was left to remember were pieces of his favorite Bible verses and lines from hymns.

Yet my grandmother—his wife for more than sixty years—traveled the road of Alzheimer's faithfully. Although she's still spunky and independent (she shocked her family by skydiving on her eighty-first birthday), she has passed up the chance to live for herself in favor of the tougher road of caring for my grandfather.

For years, she spent her time cooking, driving, bathing, wiping, lifting, and dressing my grandfather. Though I didn't recognize it at the time, now I know I was given a glimpse at one of the most beautiful sights on the entire planet: real love in action, real sacrifice. My grandmother showed me Jesus' face, hands, and feet visible in the twenty-first century. My grandmother gave herself to care for her husband, even long after the day he forgot her name.

Still, by the dictionary's definition, my grandmother did not love my grandfather. The thought of him didn't continually bring butterflies to her stomach, and at the last stage of his life my grandfather did not possess many attractive qualities. But did she love him?

In David and Alexis's story, David chased after his faithless wife. She was selfish, ungrateful, and without a single quality to make him proud to claim her. Maybe the story struck you as cheesy or unrealistic. That's fine. We live in a world where such love stories are so rare that they sound unreal. We can have a hard time believing in them. Or, maybe the cheesiness just came from my retelling— because, let me tell you, the full story of David and Alexis is as amazing as they come.

In the original, true story, the main characters have different names. Hosea was a respectable, upstanding prophet who married a less-than-respectable girl named Gomer. She had a vicious selfishness, and the person who cherished her most received only adultery in return. She ran away several times with other men, abandoning Hosea and their children. A few times she apologized to Hosea for her choices. Then she ran off again.

Real love is not fueled by emotions but by a constant desire for the good of the beloved.

One day Gomer found herself sold into slavery. She'd left the man who might've protected her, and now was destined to a life of hell. Yet Hosea, the man she had wronged the most, pursued her. He found her owner and spent his own money to purchase her freedom.

Why did Hosea still love her? How could he, when Gomer caused him so much pain? And how could my grandmother love my helpless grandfather? These are love stories that don't make sense—at least, when we look at love from the standpoint of the dictionary.

As the dictionary defines love as a weak, trembling candle, the love belonging to Hosea and to my grandmother was a steady, blazing torch. It was not fueled by emotions but by a constant desire for the good of the beloved.

Imagine a love so powerful it could shake the heavens, but also tender enough that it can caress a heart.

Wise men have said that love is a willingness to give sacrificially for another person, no matter how or if that love is returned. It means that even if the Beloved ran away or spit in Love's face, Love would still say, "I will do the most that I can to help you, always, whether you love me or not." In the words of C. S. Lewis, "Love is not affectionate feeling, but a steady wish for the loved person's ultimate good as far as it can be obtained."

I don't think Lewis meant that love is ever totally without feelings. Feelings should come hand in hand with love!

But the focus of the love isn't on how it makes the lover feel—it's on helping the beloved. Love is about serving.

Okay, now, if this is true, the world's interpretation of love is completely turned on its head. Just think—all those other causes that people pursue—admiration, respect, fame, sex, love, validity—they all fall apart. They're exposed as little "c" causes because they're all about a fake kind of love.

What then? If we no longer chase those causes, what is left for us?

Try to imagine a love even stronger than that of David's for Alexis or my grandmother's for my grandfather—a kind deeper than the distance between galaxies. Imagine a love so powerful it could shake the heavens, but also tender enough that it can caress a heart.

What kind of love is this?

It's the one that reaches for you.

I'm not kidding. Don't talk yourself out of it yet. Just let this truth seep into your bones. There really *is* love like this.

For He rescued us from the domain of darkness, and transferred us to the kingdom of His beloved Son, in whom we have redemption, the forgiveness of sins. He [Jesus] is the image of the invisible God, the firstborn of all creation. For by Him all things were created, both in the heavens and on earth . . . For it was the Father's good pleasure for all the fullness to dwell in Him, and through Him to reconcile all things to Himself, having made peace through the blood of His cross.

—COLOSSIANS 1:13–16, 19–20 NASB

CHAPTER 3

A New Definition

Darkness extended in an endless blanket of black velvet. There was nothing in sight—not a star, not a planet, not a dust particle. There was only the infinity of space spread out in a vast emptiness. No ripple of sound was heard from any living creature. No whisper of wind or movement was felt in the entire universe. All was utterly silent.

Suddenly, dazzling lights of green, yellow, blue, and billions of other nameless colors exploded like fireworks in all directions. Numberless, these new stars scattered throughout the universe, as though spread by an unseen hand. From nothing was brought forth indescribable beauty. Sheer glory was on display.

God, the Creator, was at work.

Now, take a peek into the depths of the earth, where God formed His most prized creation. His Son looked on, His face an identical reflection of the joy the Father was experiencing.

Shaped in God's very own image, this creation was special. It was close to God's heart. This creation would be His masterpiece. With the tender love of a Father and the infinite precision of a master carpenter, He crafted and carved the first man. Now, God didn't need man's companionship—or the grief that He must've known man would cause Him—but He made him anyway. He *wanted* to love him. God freely chose to bestow upon this creation the gift of being His child. It was wondrous.

Finally, God held the first man close to Himself. He breathed softly into the man His very own breath. God watched as this most beloved creation stirred to life.

Denouncing God,
human beings put something else— always something else—on His throne.

Now shift your thoughts to a wholly different scene.

An ash-gray blanket of clouds masked the sun. A grass-less hill faced the sky defiantly, its rocky ledge forming the shape of a skull. Hundreds of people swarmed the hill. They were vultures, demons with human faces. And yet their hearts beat the same as our own. All eyes stared, focused on one object. They shook their fists and chanted as a single man stumbled his way up the hill. Sweat and blood was on over the man's entire body; mechanically

he took step after step. Men mocked him and women cack-
led as metal was driven into the man's hands and feet,
shredding the muscle and igniting his limbs with pain. Hardened soldiers pulled the man's cross erect—and not too
gently.

The man's arms stretched wide, ligaments pulling and
straining, cuts stinging across his forehead, legs, and back.
Splinters from the wooden cross dug into his shoulders.
Breathe in, breathe out . . . breathe in . . . breathe . . . The weight
of his own body pressed on his lungs so much it felt like he
was being held underwater. Oh, and how thirsty he was!

Knives have been driven in the backs of many men in
history; they've even been twisted a bit for maximum pain.
Yet something caused this murder to sail above all other
crimes as the most treacherous. The knife had been driven,
but this time, it was driven into the back of God.

Thousands of years preceding the bloody scene, men
and women first drew the knife against their Creator. They
didn't simply practice evil. They became experienced pro-
fessionals in the art of treachery. Idolatry, adultery, envy,
theft, rape, murder, the love of money, rebellion, deception,
lust—human beings introduced these words to the universe. Denouncing God, they put something else—always
something else—on His throne.

The consequence? Death. Death and sin, two inseparable evils soaked their beings. It was their punishment.
These warped human souls deserved to burn in hell for
their actions.

Their Creator could have rightfully ignored them. Why not leave them to murder each other, one by one? Why not start a new race of people in some new galaxy?

I once suspected that because God is God, pain does not touch Him as it does me. Pain grabs my heart when a friend abuses my trust. If I'm overcome by feelings of betrayal, I can find it hard to breathe. We're all like that, in the face of sorrow. We hurt. We cry. We'll mourn for months and years at the loss of a loved one.

But, for some reason, I once assumed God must feel differently, that His feelings are more numb than our own.

I couldn't have been more wrong. If we're created in the image of God and our emotions are but tiny mirrors of what He must feel on an infinite scale—what must it mean for God's heart to groan in agony?

God chose to give
Love a face. The cross reminds us of how we ought to hate sin.

Earth betrayed His love. The people whose cells and mitochondria and neurons and synapses He made to function—they pretended He didn't exist. With death, they would receive their due.

But surprisingly, the Father pitied His creation. "How often I have longed to gather your children together, as a hen gathers her chicks under her wings, but you were not willing" (Matthew 23:37 NIV). Although death was mankind's reward for its actions, God intervened. He sent the Man.

During His lifetime, this Man could have set Himself up as king, taking the throne of Caesar. You wouldn't think it to look at Him hanging on a cross, but only a few days before, the entire nation had been at His feet.

He knew His power, but He did not use it against them.

When they came to crucify Him, He let them spit on His face. Why?

Because He was "God in skin." And He loved them.[1]

Could it be true? Could this wounded scarecrow of a Man really be God? We can't see too far into the past, but we do know that at our beginning, this same Man was there (Psalm 139). As God's Son—fully God Himself— He was present at the Earth's first sunrise (John 1:1–3). He was involved in the creation of the first human soul.

He was the one who had planted the tree that formed the planks that made the Cross. He was the one who had formed the hill. He had created the blood cells that seeped from His own body. He was the one who had designed and knew intimately the heart of every person who had flocked to the hill to witness the human sacrifice. This hated one, writhing in pain, was God wearing the nails of men.

Why did God choose to put on our humanity? Why did He adopt our pain and tears and death and loneliness and friendlessness and let the hurt in His own heart be compounded even more? It sounds crazy. But the Father chose a daring rescue over meting out total condemnation. Instead of across-the-board damnation, the Father sent the Man to die for men, the perfect to carry the pain of the imperfect.

He chose to give Love a face.

NO ROOM FOR APATHY

Let your mind reconsider the vastness of such love. Don't let the number of times you've heard the story lessen the shock: Jesus died for you. He gave up His life so that you could live.

It is not always easy to stare at the blood and wounds with the realization that those wounds should have been our own. But how ungrateful would we be if we refused to look at the suffering Christ endured simply because it makes us feel uncomfortable? I mean, c'mon, think about it.

A glance reminds me of this fact: we are wretched. We tend to fall for the idea that Christ died because human beings are somehow lovable. Like a bloodstained Valentine card, He just decided to be crucified to tell us of His love. But what would have been the point? If we think Christ died just to say, "I love you," we miss the big picture. There was a greater reason. He died, not because he couldn't decide between giving chocolate, roses, or crucifixion to His beloved ones—but because we *needed Him to die*.

Preacher Paul Washer once said, "People say that the Cross is a sign of how much man is worth. That is not true. The Cross is a sign of how depraved we really are."[2] If it were not for the wretchedness of our hearts, Christ would not have died. If it were not for the fact that I have lied, hated others, smart-mouthed my parents, and disobeyed my God, there would have been no reason for the Cross.

It is precisely as Jonathan Edwards preached: "Your wickedness makes you as . . . heavy as lead . . . and if God should let you go, you would immediately sink . . . .and all your righteousness would have no more influence to uphold you and keep you out of hell than a spider's web would have to stop a falling rock. Were it not that so is the sovereign pleasure of God, the earth would not bear you one moment."[3] Just *think*—that's what you are. That's what I am.

The Cross reminds us of how we ought to hate sin. There is no "middle of the road." How can I happily commit sins that I know caused the death of God? How can I continue to lie, hate, lust, and steal when I know how much they cost Him?

Jesus preached, "Repent, for the kingdom of heaven is at hand" (Matthew 4:17 ESV). The word for "repent" in the original Greek is *metanoao*, which means an "abhorrence of one's previous actions and a desire to make amends."[4] So repentance is more than just an apology. It means hating our past actions and wanting to turn our backs on those actions completely.

The Cross reminds me that my sins died with Christ that day. I must now live without them. Sin must be fought tooth and nail to keep it from gaining any of my affections. The love of Christ is what controls me now.

IT'S REAL LOVE

Let me pursue a tangent here. I've gotta say this, because it's something I've fought to understand for a long time. I want to lift you up with these "field notes" from my own months upon months of struggling with this concept.

Acknowledging your unworthiness does not downplay the love God has for you. God doesn't love you less because you're a sinner. In fact, the opposite is true. Christ's love for us is much more amazing when we realize how undeserving we are.

The same hands that wove you together were pierced through and hung limp by the nails you earned. The same lungs that breathed life into billions were breathless—lifeless—because of you. It was God's decision.

What was the reward for the pain He endured? You. You are His prize. You're part of the joy set before Him that helped Him press on. The love He harbors for you is boundless.

Remember your most recent sinful thought? Remember the last time you were tempted and gave in? Wasn't it . . . like . . . five minutes ago?

Let's face it: we're not the most logical friends of a

God most holy. Even when God specifically calls our hearts to do something good, we twist and squirm at the thought. We're about as unlovable as we could be.

And still, He loves us. He loves you.

Just soak in that thought. Are you shuddering under its glory as I am right now?

This is a hard truth to wrap our minds around sometimes, because we tend to view God either as a puppy dog begging for our love or as a tyrant forcing our affection. Neither comparison is true. God is not a tyrant. God is not a puppy.

You are Christ's prize.
The gospel is God Himself.

God is unlike anything we've ever known. God doesn't love the way people do. He doesn't love us based on our attractiveness. He doesn't love us based on our goodness (we don't have any). And He doesn't love us because we loved Him first. God's love is mysterious. We may see hints of it in the world—in steadfast, caring marriages or even in undying friendships—but God's love is a higher concentrate than anything else we could imagine.

He chose to love you long before you ever dreamed of calling out to Him. Actually, the Bible says God chose you before time existed (Ephesians 1:4). Before days were days,

His love for you was already ancient.

Although God could be completely happy without you and He doesn't need you at all, He wants you. He wants you so much we could almost say He wants you desperately, though even that word doesn't quite fit. It makes more sense to say that He loves you fiercely. The Lion of justice has sworn His love for you and me—the unjust.

THIS IS HOW CHANGE FEELS

Of course, the Lion has also made a lot of enemies, if only because he possessed teeth. In His time on earth, Jesus rocked the boat. No one could understand how this carpenter from Nazareth could tell such vivid, meaningful stories and explain Scripture that had mystified even the Ivy League educated of His day. He physically tossed out the marketers and businessmen from the temple, who were busily cashing in on the industry of holiness. He told the rich to sell all they had and live for God's kingdom. He told the poor they needed to leave their families and whatever tied their hearts to the ground. His boldness both startled and frightened the country's leaders, but it was His love that was most confusing.

A walking contradiction, Jesus had the potential for great political power, yet He chose to dine with cheats, liars, the sick, and the lowest in society. When the popular, intellectually brilliant rabbi stooped down to take little children into His arms, Jesus' identity became a stunning mystery.

And His person called for a response. Sam Storms wrote in his book *One Thing*, "Apathy is impossible in the presence of the Son of God. Ineffable beauty compels a response: either passionate devotion or hatred. Middle-of-the-road, straddle-the-fence, you-do-your-thing-and-I'll-do-mine indifference dies when Jesus draws near. Love him or despise him, but abandon . . . [the myth] that he can be tolerated. Sing for joy or spit in his face. Apathy simply isn't an option."[5] The reality of Jesus poses a paradox, a question, a challenge. A Cause.

Jesus shattered assumptions when He walked the earth, and He shattered mine. He opened my eyes to truth, and I have never been the same.

As I said before, one of my greatest struggles has always been in the area of beauty. Even as a little girl, love and beauty, in my mind, were always braided together. I always wanted to be beautiful because I thought that would eventually bring me love.

Yet as time passed and the more I compared myself to the beauty of others, the less I found myself measuring up. There are so many drop-dead gorgeous girls in the world, I knew I didn't stand a chance.

Then a Jewish Carpenter came on the scene. I knew He healed people with leprosy and held little children in His lap, but I was most convinced of His power when He spoke about hope to me. It wasn't all that mystical—He didn't appear before me in a vision. I heard His voice in different ways—mostly from the Bible, but also in prayer as Scripture came back to silence the other voices in my head.

He explained that love isn't really love if it must be earned. If I had to look like a model in order for someone to love me, then His care for me was only temporary. I cheapened love by mistaking it with selfish desires. I had been stupid.

Jesus said this about love, and the Cross proved it: "Greater love has no one than this, that someone lay down his life for his friends" (John 15:13). Love is sacrifice. Love is constancy.

Jesus gives us both sacrifice and constancy. As love asks for only love in return, He calls us to follow Him.

This is not "following" a la Facebook or Twitter. It's not a click of a button. Following Him is agreeing with God that He should overhaul our lives. And then He proceeds with the overhaul—ripping out the rotting parts and grafting in new ones in one constant operation that will endure for the rest of our lives.

The discipleship He demands isn't cheap or easy. But He deserves it.

There is a hymn that speaks of "surveying the wondrous Cross." The hymn writer was bewildered at the mystery before him, proclaiming that "love so amazing, love divine, demands my heart, my soul, my all."

Is God really worthy of our all?

Well, let me ask the question this way: Does a former

slave love her emancipator? Does she feel grateful at all to the one who unclasped the chains from her hands and feet? Um, yes. How could she not?

How then can we not love the One who saved us from oh-so-much more?

Christ's action on our behalf demands a response—and not a quiet little whimper of a "thank-You." He deserves a lung-splitting cry of "Jesus, I am Yours completely!"

The gospel isn't only the agonizing pain that Christ endured on the Cross. It is broader than that. The gospel is God Himself, the gift and joy of being able to know Him—Jesus, God the Father, the Holy Spirit—the One our souls were made to love. The gospel is the drama of the trinity and glory unveiled.

Whether we realize it or not, we each have a door before us. We have seen our deserved punishment and our Cross become His. The question must now be asked: Are we ready to give Christ our all—to allow our assumptions, perceptions, and, eventually, our lives to be transformed?[6]

Will we make Him our Cause?

There are two ways

to be your own Savior and Lord. One is by breaking all the moral laws and setting your own course, and one is by keeping all the moral laws and being very, very good.

—TIM KELLER

Please Drill
This into
My Head

AN INTERJECTION

I recently came to an interesting conclusion about myself: I'm a legalist. If you're not familiar with Christianity or "Christianese," you should know that legalism is basically on par with a cuss word in Christian circles. You never, ever want to be called a legalist. It's the kiss of death.

I used to think being a legalist meant being a stodgy, close-minded moralist, like the man in the three-piece suit who's a longtime elder at his church but stomps his boot down at the idea of any newfangled outreach programs. A legalist is supposedly the person who refuses to sing anything but Gregorian chants. A legalist is old fashioned. A legalist says God only votes a certain way. A legalist is not . . . *me.*

We do things to make ourselves feel holier, to soothe our consciences, or to make ourselves feel more worthy before God.

At least, that's how I used to define it. Of course, I considered myself immune. I was a hipster compared to the guy in the three-piece suit (though real hipsters would probably laugh at me). Surely that word, "legalism," would never apply.

Legalism is the desire to earn God's love by doing good things.

You can tell what's coming. "If a man thinks he stands, he should beware lest he fall," right? (1 Corinthians 1:10). Yeah. Right.

If I am honest about myself, I realize that I'm a hard-core legalist. I make a hymns-only lady look like a novice. I do things all the time because they make me feel like a better person, to uplift my sense of superiority and self-esteem. I use good works like steroids to pump up my ego—not out of a heart genuinely wanting to serve Christ.

Legalism isn't so much the grouchy-old-man image we so often assign it. The real thing is far more sinister. Legalism is the desire to calm our sense of guilt and earn God's love by doing good things. It's clinging to a set of rules to convince ourselves that we are holy, while forgetting our need for God's mercy and forgiveness.

This definition fits me. For instance, if I pick up an abandoned shopping cart in a parking lot and begin to push it back to the grocery store, I'm usually whining in my

head about the obviously self-centered, careless person
who ditched it there. That, or I'm thinking about how
many germs are on the shopping cart's handle. But usually
it's the first one.

If I say something nice or smile at the homeless guy on
the corner, I usually think disparagingly of all the other
people who've walked by and ignored the homeless guy.

If you're like me, the good stuff you do isn't typically
the result of a heart just oozing with compassion. We do
things to make ourselves feel righteous to soothe our consciences, or to make ourselves feel more worthy before
God. Even our good actions often originate in pompous-
ness—or legalism.

Glorifying Jesus
is the only reason we are alive.

That's why it's iffy when people start prescribing
"wholesome Christian behavior" or repping self-help books.
I don't need training to become a bigger, better legalist, to
have a more fortified sense of self-righteousness. I'm pretty
sure there's a reason God didn't title the Bible, *Six Easy
Steps to a Happy Life.*

He's in the business of hearts and souls.

It's amazing how many Jesus-followers—genuine,

works-in-progress children of God—put undue focus on having "Christian" behavior, when the Bible itself offers a different view.

It's not about what you do.

Jesus says, it's about whom you do it for.

My pastor, Matt Chandler, once said, "There's nothing more exhausting than not having genuine affection for Jesus Christ and trying to obey all the rules." If you try to be a Jesus-follower by doing all the "right" things without loving Him at all, you'll feel like a triangular peg trying to fit into a circular hole. It won't work. You'll feel depressed and exasperated.

Even if you *are* a redeemed sinner, if you obey only out of habit or because you think you can earn God's appreciation, you'll end up feeling pretty rotten because you're trying to push behavior change that can only come from contact with a supernatural power—*without* the supernatural power.

That's why I wanted to talk to you first about the Cause that has taken its hold on my heart (and hopefully on yours as well). What I didn't want to do was review a list of behavior changes, things we should or shouldn't do as Christians.

Simply put, glorifying Jesus is the only reason we are alive. The. Only. Reason. We've got to love and know and glorify Him! And the mercy He lavishes on you is the only way you have to know Him. You have nothing to stand on—no good works you do (or bad stuff you don't do) will impress God. All you have is grace.

Here's where Dietrich Bonhoeffer, the German theologian, would interrupt me, "But, but, but—that's not all! You can't totally *disregard* obedience in the name of grace!" And I agree. There's another side to this coin. God isn't impressed by our good works, but He still calls us to do them. After all, how can we be adopted by God's Cause but never champion it? How can we be saved by grace from our sins and still blissfully flirt with that same sin? It'd be like a person who has been bitten by a rattlesnake and given antivenin, but who then goes back to cuddle with the snake as if nothing had happened.

The venerable Bonhoeffer interjects, "'Cheap grace' is the preaching of forgiveness without requiring repentance [or heart change]."[1] What Bonhoeffer called "cheap grace" is trying to accept the forgiveness of Christ without actually following Him; it's trying to take the gift of salvation that Jesus gives to those who worship Him without actually worshipping Him.

Jesus didn't mince words on this topic either.

"If anyone would come after me, let him deny himself and take up his cross and follow me. For whoever would save his life will lose it, but whoever loses his life for my sake and the gospel's will save it. For what does it profit a man to gain the whole world and forfeit his soul? For what can a man give in return for his soul? For whoever is ashamed of me and of my words in this adulterous and sinful generation, of him will the Son of Man also be ashamed when he comes in the glory of his Father with the holy angels" (Mark 8:34–38).

So while legalists like me need a motive overhaul, we still have no excuse for disobedience. If you say you follow the Cause, your actions need to back up what you say.

Let's not have a communication breakdown. I want us to be clear that, in the next few chapters, what I say shouldn't be taken like a medical prescription. In other words, I don't want to simply give a list of ten things you should and shouldn't do to live a God-honoring life. Rather, I want to provide a springboard. As I've written these chapters, my understanding of what God wants from me deepened and stretched. My hope is that your understanding will deepen and stretch as you read—not because *I* open your eyes, but because God has decided to use words written by a girl with her own flaws and weaknesses to illuminate a principle He wants you to learn.

That said, the next few chapters (spoiler alert—in case you're dying to know what's next) are about the things we're called to do as disciples of Christ. We're going to kick at the little "c" causes that so often snag our feet, and try to replace them with a Jesus-centered view. The following chapter about beauty will explore our underlying cultural assumptions and counter them with Scripture. Then we'll explore purity versus promiscuity (or if you dislike alliteration, sex and saying no. Not that I didn't just alliterate there, too!).

I've tried to pick topics that most people are quick to

ignore and that our culture finds really foreign. So these chapters should be fun if you really like thinking independently. However, *even biblical behaviors can quickly turn into little "c" causes themselves that distract from the main Cause, if we lose sight of the Reason for our obedience.*

Without love, these acts of obedience won't make sense. Without the gospel, we'll become legalists. But if we keep coming back to Jesus as the central reason for these changes, we'll keep that bad word *legalism* at bay.

Don't worry. If we stay close to Jesus, we'll be fine.

. . . of her, and every

created thing I praise, I should say "in some way, in its unique way, [is] like Him who made it."

—C. S. LEWIS, *A Grief Observed*

CHAPTER 4

The Beauty Cause

It must have been about two in the morning, and I was sleeping over at my friend Daria's house. We decided we'd prefer to keep chatting than actually sleep (of course). We came up with a game idea, and convinced ourselves it was brilliant. The game? "Philosophizing." The point was to argue about a topic neither of us knew anything about . . . and win. (Yes, I know. Geeky!)

I came up with the first topic. "Okay, Dar. Here's the question: 'What is beauty?'"

She rolled her eyes. "Great. *You* pick a hard question, and *I'm* supposed to answer it?"

"Basically . . . yes."

"Okay. Do you want me to define beauty in people or in things?"

"Define it in . . ." I struggled for a challenging subject. My eyes caught the pencil holder on Daria's desk, which gave me an idea. "Define beauty in a pair of scissors."

"Scissors *aren't* beautiful!" she cried indignantly.

"How do you know? What makes a pair of scissors beautiful?"

Daria grabbed the pair of scissors on her desk. "They're . . . uh . . . scissors are beautiful . . . because of how well they function."

Suddenly, we both had a lightbulb moment: "So if scissors work the way their maker wanted them to work, then they're beautiful?"

Let's unpack that. The value of a pair of scissors isn't based on its sleek design. It's based on whether it pleases the person who designed it. I don't care if my scissors are pink or yellow. I think they're perfect when the hinge isn't rusted and the blades are sharp enough to cut paper.

Although most conversations at two in the morning are without substance, my friend and I stumbled on a key truth that applies to far more than a pair of scissors. It is a truth that affects every one of us and has the potential to change lives. What is it? Our Maker's opinion.

Are you feeling confused? "What? Scissors? How do scissors have anything to do with people, or real life for that matter?" Though I promise you that scissors do pertain, we must first step back and take a look at how we gauge beauty in creations far more important than scissors: human beings.

JUST YOUR AVERAGE MISS UNIVERSE

In 1883, Sir Francis Galton developed the "Theory of Averageness." While then he was called a "scientist," today we'd call Sir Francis a total racist. He was a proponent of eugenics and the idea that human beings should be bred carefully in order to produce a smarter, superhuman generation. Basically, he was a creeper—or maybe a really shortsighted "scientist"—who didn't see the disasters his ideology would help bring about, such as the Holocaust. (As an interesting note of trivia, Sir Francis was a cousin of Charles Darwin. Their family tree has nothing to do with this example, but if that info one day wins you big on *Jeopardy*, I'd like a cut of the check, please.)

So why am I calling Sir Francis a creeper? Well, not only did he create an image of what he thought the "typical" Jewish person looked like, he also stereotyped criminals. He assumed that all criminals might share common characteristics—like squinty eyes or cleft chins.[1]

We grow accustomed to an idea of how faces "should" look, and when we meet a face that doesn't fit the mold, we label it as "unattractive."

If his idea were true, we could judge a person's character by looking at her face. This would be of endless value to police officers, and even to the common person who wanted to distinguish a shady car salesman from an honest one.

Sir Francis never found proof for his theory. In fact, it is considered today to be utterly false. Criminals don't look alike. However, in the process of his experimentation, he did discover something fascinating about the human view of beauty.

Using the limited technology of his time, Sir Francis blurred together headshots of multiple male criminals until he came up with a single picture. This picture, he supposed, would represent the face of the "average criminal." The result was a face that was surprisingly . . . handsome.

Though Sir Francis failed in his theory, he did spark an idea. Further scientific study, undertaken years later, suggests that people who are considered "beautiful" or "handsome" often share the same traits. It's not unusual for them to have a similar face shape, nose length, etc. An averaging together of the 2005 Miss Universe contestants reveals that it was extremely common for competitors to have narrow noses, high cheekbones, and wide smiles. Some of the Miss Universe composite images even look like identical twins.[2]

What's the point of this research? It means that our brains determine that some people are attractive exactly because they are average! We find faces pretty when they look so very *normal*. We grow accustomed to an idea of how faces "should" look, and when we meet a face that doesn't fit the mold, we label it as "unattractive." "Beautiful" faces are those that remind us of others like them.

Our American Beauty
checklist is not a concrete thing but an ever-changing standard.

The flip side to this research is the nature of "ugliness." What if people are considered less attractive simply because they look different? Not because they are actually lacking in intrinsic beauty—but because they don't fit into our mental picture of what is beautiful.

Let's stop and consider that. Have you ever met someone who was deformed from birth? What made that person's face stand out from other faces? They were *not* average. In fact, they were incredibly unique.

While the Theory of Averageness may or may not be completely accurate in describing the way people look at beauty, it does pose some interesting ideas: What if people we consider unattractive are actually *extraordinary*? What if beautiful people are not really any better designed than the rest? What if what we commonly call "beauty" depends solely on our point of view?

THE BEAUTY CHECKLIST

Whether or not we're conscious of the fact, when given the task of judging a person's looks, we compare them to a mental list. Large eyes, small noses, thin waists, toned arms, long legs, pouty lips, arched eyebrows, hair that doesn't frizz or get stringy, skin clear of blemishes and freckles, ears that lay close to the head, and so on—this "Beauty Checklist" is just off the top of my head. It's basically what our culture considers beautiful (with exceptions, of course).

If you and I grew up on an island with only a few other inhabitants, without a single lifeline to civilization, we probably wouldn't naturally think up this checklist. We'd most likely have a completely different list of attractive features.

Our surroundings determine how we think. Growing up on a remote island would probably greatly affect our views of beauty. Our opinions would not have been influenced by American culture via friends, movies, magazines, and makeup companies. Our perspective would be radically different.

Prettiness isn't universal. Not every culture agrees that deep tans are attractive or that slenderness is an important part of beauty (which should make us question why we cling to such wavering standards and subject ourselves to worry because we don't "fit"). Pale, white skin is held in high esteem in China. A woman is praised if she is heavy in South Africa. Standards of beauty differ. Cultures across the world disagree with the American Beauty Checklist of attractive qualities.

My family and I experienced this firsthand several years ago on a trip to Japan. Out of a family of brown-eyed brunettes, Tyler, my younger brother, was the only one to be born with green eyes and blond curls. At home, this difference did not matter much. But weaving through a bustling Japanese marketplace or a packed subway station where most heads were topped with dark brown or black hair, Tyler was a mini-celebrity.

Young and old women alike covered their mouths to giggle at his cuteness. On some occasions, strangers ran their hands through his curls or asked for a photo. One elderly woman even smothered my brother's face with kisses. He still blushes about that one.

Today as an American on American soil, if you happen to have the guts to run your fingers through my brother's hair, he'll be shocked and completely disturbed. If you weren't a girl, he'd probably hit you. Unlike in Japan, Americans don't kiss the face of strangers simply because their hair is blond. Here in the United States, blond hair isn't a rarity and is, therefore, not prized. These differences around the world show that our American Beauty Checklist is not a concrete thing but an ever-changing standard.

Even in the United States, the idea of what is beautiful has evolved over the years. In the 1940s, actresses would completely shave or pluck their eyebrows to pencil in fake versions. Yet a mere forty years later, in the 1980s, the trend was to allow eyebrows to grow thick and long.

In spite of the changes in the Beauty Checklist throughout history and the world, young women often compare themselves to this list to find their status. (I wonder, did you find yourself comparing your body to the checklist when I first mentioned it?) Those lucky few who reach each of the standards are then labeled as "beautiful," and those who don't find themselves described by the checklist end up feeling they must content themselves with being less than the best.

It is incredibly dangerous when we make beauty our cause.

Buying into these principles is disastrous, both for those who are considered beautiful *and* for those who are not. "Beautiful" girls must work at remaining on top. This may include dieting and the stress of keeping people's approval. "Less attractive" girls must work to achieve beauty, also dieting and spending time before the mirror. The goal for both is to gain admirers. "If other people approve of your looks, then you're pretty. This," says the culture, "is beauty." Welcome to the world.

Nevertheless, if my friend Daria and I were right, and scissors are valuable when they bring satisfaction to their maker, why must we compare ourselves to the Beauty

Checklist at all? Why doesn't the same rule go for us as the scissors?

I think it does.

A SECOND OPINION

Let's compare two sixteen-year-old girls for a moment. Chloe is shy and tenderly nicknamed "the Mouse" by her family. She's never been popular and certainly would never gain friends on account of her looks. Her frizzy black hair is uncontrollable, and her round, pale face is what some might call "plain." Callie, on the other hand, is confident, outgoing, and witty. Her address book is as thick as a phonebook. Popularity has never been a problem for her. Her face smacks of stardom. Even on a day without her morning coffee, Callie's eyes are bright and sparkling.

Which would you rate as beautiful, Callie or Chloe? What is more, which would God rate as beautiful? Looking at the Bible, the answer is straightforward: "So God created man in his own image, *in the image of God he created him*; male *and* female he created them. . . . And God saw everything that he had made, and behold, it was *very* good" (Genesis 1:27, 31, italics mine). And in Psalm 139:13–14 (NIV), the creation process is also described: "For you created my inmost being; you knit me together in my mother's womb. I praise you because I am fearfully and wonderfully made; your works are wonderful, I know that full well."

Before Callie and Chloe were infants, wheeled from

their moms' hospital beds, placed in strollers, and put on display for admiring relatives to "ooo" and "aah" over, God had already decided they were valuable. He approved of the way He had formed them, from their tiny baby fingernails to the fuzz atop their heads.

"Shrink that waist, girl! Diet, diet, diet! Want to be loved, honey?" The world issues demands like a drill sergeant. "Pluck those eyebrows. Style that hair. If you want to be valued as a human being, change yourself!" The world longs to twist Callie, Chloe, and the rest of us to reflect its own image, to make us bow at the altar of what it calls "beauty."

To make matters clear—I'm not saying it's wrong to pluck your eyebrows or style your hair. Hygiene is definitely *not* a bad thing. But it is incredibly dangerous when we make beauty our cause. When we obsess over faces, hair, and style, we threaten to waste our lives. We risk coming to the end of existence with nothing to show for it except the scant moments we felt pretty.

The beauty obsession also can make us forget that the world is dead wrong. Overlooking the masterpiece that is each human being, the world's criticisms are like an architect swaggering around the pyramids of Giza, saying, "No one likes buildings in that outdated style anymore. Pyramids are so *yesterday*. Let's knock 'em down and build a skyscraper instead."

When the bulldozers come, I'll be among the first to picket in front of the pyramids. Their destruction would be a travesty, because even though they're unusual, they're marvelous wonders of the world.

The same could be said of the human body. You are timeless. God didn't make your body in order to please what some fashion magazine decided was attractive. You were designed to reflect God's *own* image. To disregard your design is to commit a greater injustice than demolishing the pyramids.

Look at your hair. God chose that color for you. Your fingers—God chose their size. Genes may have chosen your nose, but God chose your genes. Your body was His idea. Like the pair of scissors, we were made with a specific function in mind. The design God gave our bodies is perfect to carry out His purpose.

In her book *Let Me Be a Woman*, Elisabeth Elliot tells of Gladys, a young woman who realized this truth:

When . . . [Gladys Aylward] was a child she had two great sorrows. One, that while all of her friends had beautiful golden hair, hers was black. The other, that while her friends were still growing, she stopped. She was about four feet ten inches tall. But when at last she reached the country to which God had called her to be a missionary, she stood on the wharf in Shanghai and looked around at the people to whom He called her.

"Every single one of them," she said, "had black hair. And every single one of them had stopped growing when I did. And I said, 'Lord God, You know what You're doing!' "[3]

While at the time, China was extremely closed off to Western influence, Gladys was uniquely equipped to share the gospel with them because she did not have the intimidating height or blue eyes often associated with foreigners. Her looks, although a source of grief when she was a girl, proved to be a part of God's greater plan for her life.

It may be hard to believe at times, especially when we look in the mirror first thing in the morning, but our looks are not accidental. God didn't just grab a fistful of dust, stick it in the blender, and say "Presto!" and the human race was born. He created us with tender care. Regardless of what others think, in the eyes of our Creator, we were wonderfully made.

While we may never figure out, as Gladys Aylward did, the reason for our hair type or height, we can be certain that God has a purpose for our appearance and not a single feature was a mistake. We are not valued because we win beauty contests but because God made us. Every freckle, hair, and mole was created by God for a reason—if only for His pleasure.

PRACTICALLY SPEAKING: MAKEUP

So beauty shouldn't trip us up anymore. It's one of the lesser causes we would be stupid to pursue (speaking as someone who has been that stupid!). But how should we relate to beauty correctly? I mean, we could ditch it altogether and wear potato sacks, but is that really necessary? I don't think so! After all, in its purest state, beauty was invented by God. He wants us to enjoy beauty and the loveliness He's put everywhere.

Still, my answers aren't cut and dried on this question; I'm still working through it myself. But on the subject of makeup in particular, I've gleaned some opinions from wise friends that you might find thought-provoking.

For nearly a year, my mom and I lived in dread of my two younger sisters saying these six words: "Can I give you a makeover?" The question came almost daily, with my mom the most obliging victim.

My sisters, Grace and Miriam, would take turns creatively rearranging Mom's face. A moment with a cosmetic pencil would result in a caterpillar-like eyebrow stretching across her forehead. Pink lipstick, they found, produced better results than blush. You can imagine how their "projects" ended up looking like Picassos.

My sisters have since grown out of their "makeover" stage, but when I meet women who hide their faces behind a sheet of makeup, I am occasionally reminded of their juvenile sense of style.

Tell me, why, oh why, women feel the need to cover their faces with makeup as if they were masks! Why does it seem necessary to disguise wrinkles and skin tones with layers of powder upon concealer upon foundation and more concealer? How is that more beautiful than the unmasked version?

I love what a mother I know says to her daughters

when they put on too much makeup. She likes to remind them that they are "painting butterflies" with mascara and shadow. No one would dream of painting over a butterfly's colors, and yet sometimes we do just that to ourselves.

I'm not saying we should toss our makeup cases in the garbage. I wear makeup. Lipstick, eyeliner, eyeshadow, blush, powder, foundation, mascara—I've used it all and don't think it's wrong. But when makeup ceases to accent the face and begins to cover the natural beauty God made, then it reflects the mixed-up priorities of the wearer.

I appreciate what writer Bethany Patchin-Torode expressed:

There's nothing wrong with a woman occasionally high-lighting her features with makeup. But it's doubtful that God wants us to spend half the morning covering up the faces he intentionally blessed us with. There is a certain honesty and vulnerability in a clean, unembellished face. It shows humility, and draws attention away from the merely external to the soul shining through the eyes. There's also nothing inherently bad about a man working out to strengthen his muscles. But spending hours in the gym striving for perfectly defined tone is not a good use of one's time or body. There is much more to be admired in the modest arms of a man who increases his strength by carrying his children, tilling the ground, or maintaining his house. The Apostle Paul calls the body the temple of the Holy

Spirit. We should worship with the temple; we must not worship the temple itself. The body is a glorious creation, but its purpose is to glorify the Creator.[4]

PRACTICALLY SPEAKING: FASHION

Okay, what of fashion? Can a girl be interested in looking stylish without being vain? And how much interest is too much interest? To answer these questions, I asked Christa Taylor.

Christa is a bubbly twentysomething living in the outskirts of Portland, Oregon. She stepped into the fashion industry at the age of nineteen when she launched her own clothing brand. But Christa's business is different from most.

While many of her outfits are chic (Michelle Obama, Audrey Hepburn, and Jackie O are some of Christa's favorite style icons), they boldly stand away from the crowd. They're modest. Of Christa's skirts, tops, and swimsuits, there isn't a plunging neckline or bared stomach among them. (If you don't know what to make of modesty, be patient. The topic is coming up in a couple chapters.)

That's the "official" résumé. As a friend, I can testify to Christa's nature. She's not quiet or mousy by any stretch of the imagination. She doesn't wear modest clothes so she can "hide away" from the world. Christa is who she is because of a conscious choice. She's coined the term "empowered traditionalist"; it means she's an admirer of smart, feminine beauty. To Christa, modesty takes priority over edginess, but fashion still goes before frump.

When I heard back from Christa for this interview, she had just finished another photo shoot. Her excitement was tangible. "Fashion is, to me, an art form," she explained, "another way of me expressing my creative individuality."

Hmm, so did Christa think it possible to enjoy fashion while not obsessing over one's image? "Yes!" she responded emphatically. "While we must constantly be on guard against our sinful desires—for attention from the guys and a competitive edge with the girls—I sincerely believe you can emulate the beauty and creativity of Christ through the way you dress." Then she added, "Let's face it—fashion is fun. As long as we keep it in proper balance, I think the Lord is honored when we delight in new and creative fashions."

And what exactly is a "proper balance"? "It starts in the heart," says Christa. "If I find I'm dressing to attract attention or be the most stylish girl present, or even if I wear something that pushes the envelope and draws all the attention to my outward appearance—that is going too far. We are to be primarily known, not for our good looks or name-brand clothing, but our good works."

God has given us a natural, human, and particularly female love for beauty. We love pretty things. It's not wrong to love what's beautiful, and when we're not looking to earn the adoration of others, fashion can be an outlet for creativity—creativity not unlike the creative nature of God.

WHY IT MATTERS

To summarize this chapter, it's helpful for me to look at my feet. Or more specifically, it helps to look at my toes. Not only do they still boast scars from my days of playing hockey as a little kid, they're long, skinny, and not at all pretty. I could never be a foot model. Even my dad has always noted how "weird" my feet are (he can say this safely because they look like his).

Thanks to what I know about God, in spite of knowing my feet are "weird," I'm at peace with wearing sandals. If God is satisfied to create me this way, shouldn't I be satisfied to *be* this way? Shouldn't I rest in knowing He thought these feet would work for me just fine? After all, this is isn't some fashion magazine editor approving my feet. It's God, and God loves the way I'm made.

Wait a second. You might have just read that sentence with disgust. Maybe you're a really smart, skeptical person who is currently thinking up some edgy sarcastic comment: "So God thinks I'm special. Woo-hoo. What a surprise. Let's all hold hands and sing 'Kumbaya' now because we're all at peace with how God made us. C'mon. What's the point?"

All right, kid, the gig is up. If that is what you were thinking—I understand perfectly. To some, "God loves the way you're made" sounds like a sappy line from a greeting card. We've all heard it before, that God created us and loves us, and it held no meaning then. Knowing those

words did not stop the world from pressuring us to change
our bodies. The phrase never really made a difference.
Why should we care now? Why should it carry weight
now?

This truth *doesn't* carry any special weight . . .

Unless we remember who God is.

If we remember that He is the Almighty Creator of
every single human being, then His approval makes a difference. If we remember that when we reach the grave and
the voices of magazines, movies, and music die out, His is
the only opinion that ever will matter or ever truly mattered, then it makes a difference. If we remember that
"the Lord tests hearts" (Proverbs 17:3)—He knows our
every motive—then we have a great reason for the respect-
ful consideration of His opinion.

My feet are a ridiculous example of how obsessed we
can be about every detail of our bodies looking "beautiful."
I'm sure we all have our own "toe problems," or aspects of
our body that we are tempted to be self-conscious about,
but let's run away from that temptation as fast as our ugly
feet can carry us. Forget about your "flaws." If we think on
the subject too much, we'll run the risk of being distracted
from a much, much, much greater issue.

Give him the glory, for the marriage of the Lamb has come, and his Bride has made herself ready; it was granted her to clothe herself with fine linen, bright and pure—for the fine linen is the righteous deeds of the saints.

—REVELATION 19:7–8

Nothing is yet in its true form.

—C. S. LEWIS, *Till We have Faces*

Is this a soul that stirs in me?/ Is it breaking free, wanting to come alive?/ 'Cause my comfort would prefer for me to be numb/And avoid the impending birth of who I was born to become.

—BROOKE FRASER, singer-songwriter

CHAPTER 5

Deeper
Than Skin

"It's funny you're writing this book, Hannah."

We were standing in a coffee shop. I had just told my friend "Danielle" about the book I was writing (the one in your hands) when a strange look spread across her face. She glanced at the floor and then around the coffee shop to ensure no one was listening. Leaning her hand against the countertop, she stared me squarely in the eyes. Then she said, "You know, *I* was bulimic."

Self-conscious, she searched my face for a reaction. I must've looked surprised. Never in a million years would I have suspected anything so deep and painful troubled Danielle.

As a disgustingly talented musician with dark hair and gray-blue eyes, most girls would find her face and talents enviable. Plus Danielle seems constantly to have a smile on her face. No one would ever suspect her of having grief or depression. I could hardly believe her confession.

"You?" I blinked.

"Yeah. I made myself vomit all the time, thinking it would make me lose weight. It wasn't until my mom caught me one day that my family found out . . . " Her voice trailed away. Then she went on. "Of course, you know that the vomiting and stress often make you *gain* weight, not lose it. Bulimia is totally pointless, but it's also . . . hard to describe."

Maybe it was in her voice or her face—I don't know—but for that fleeting moment, I noticed a brokenness about Danielle I had never seen before.

While we may think our problems stem from "self-esteem" issues, I suspect half of our issues stem from too much self-esteem.

She looked away. "My sisters had never done anything quite like it. They still don't really understand." She paused again. Turning to face me, she enunciated slowly: "I was *completely obsessed with myself.* Really, bulimia is one of the most *selfish* things you can do."

Danielle was speaking almost exactly the same words I had heard from another friend, "Jasmine," a former anorexic. Jasmine had spoken almost angrily of the pain she had brought upon herself: "You know, not only is anorexia *stupid* because you're destroying your body's natural metabolism . . . it's *selfish.*"

In case you've ever wondered, take it from those who've already walked that road: eating disorders don't bring happiness. I wish I could express all the emotion that crossed Danielle's face, but I honestly can't. Just imagine the face of one of the most joyful people you know transitioning to visible pain.

As Danielle and Jasmine proved, it's not enough simply to believe God created your body fearfully and wonderfully. They both had heard (and probably memorized) that psalm, but their eyes were turned inward. Danielle and Jasmine still were susceptible to eating disorders because for them—and for us—self-focus comes naturally.

If we're honest, the problem we girls face with beauty is *not* that we don't know our bodies are created wonderfully by God. We know that. The problem isn't even so much Photoshop, plastic surgery, Barbie, or magazines either, though these things create the perfect environment to encourage us in our beauty obsession. Part of the problem can be our own self-focus. While we may think our problems stem from self-esteem issues, I suspect that half of our issues stem from too much self-esteem. We mentally evaluate and condemn and criticize our bodies because we're obsessed with *ourselves* and worry that we could possibly be physically "imperfect."

This is not in any way to invalidate the struggles of those with eating disorders. Obsessing about myself is something I've struggled with countless times, and still do. Obviously, there are other factors that play into those struggles as well—whether psychological troubles or past experiences. Just the same, we need to be aware of the connection between self-focus and mental illnesses. One can feed the other.

The only way, then, to escape the beauty obsession is to become obsessed with something else—something truly worth it.[1]

LAST WORDS

He did not cry easily, but the sight of his friends—more like brothers—gathering around him in prayer for the last time was enough to bring Paul to tears. For three years they had struggled side by side, proclaiming the gospel to the stubborn city of Ephesus. Together the band of brothers had shouldered the threat of beatings, imprisonment, and even death from those hostile to their message.

We aren't supposed to draw security from belonging to Christ and have the experience end there.

With each brother he'd developed a strong bond. Paul distinctly remembered nights when he had remained awake into the early morning hours, kneeling in prayer for every one of the men. Now he was leaving them. He was making the journey to Jerusalem alone.

In his spirit, Paul knew this was the last he would see of them in this lifetime.

Paul's last message to the Ephesian men is interesting. Naturally, it would contain his heart's cry—what truth he wanted most for these men to cling to:

> I do not account my life of any value nor as precious to myself, if only I may finish my course and the ministry that I received from the Lord Jesus, to testify to the gospel of the grace of God. . . . In all things I have shown you that by working hard in this way we must help the weak and remember the words of the Lord Jesus, how He Himself said, "It is more blessed to give than to receive." (Acts 20:24, 35)

The point Paul so desperately wanted to convey to these dear friends was not that God loved them. They knew the gospel. They recognized God's supreme love in sending His Son. What they needed to hear most from Paul was this final challenge: *Don't value yourself.*

Paul's goal was not to lift their self-esteem. "I do not account my life of any value," he wrote. Rather, he hoped to lift their eyes to Christ.

The key words spoken by Paul were not meant only for the ears of his Ephesian buddies. God means those words for us, too. We aren't supposed to draw security from belonging to Christ and have the experience *end* there.

God's love for us should not drive us to higher self-esteem but instead to a higher value of His opinion.

Once I'm set free from constantly trying to mimic the clothes and faces and body types of everyone else, I'm really, really free! It makes me want to dance around with a permanent marker and paint moustaches on all the little images I've had stored in my mind of what I "should" look like. No longer must I appease these images in an attempt to be loved, because my Maker loves me as I am!

But that's not all. In fact, if learning about God's love *ended* at elevating my self-esteem, I'd only be worshiping myself. Christ would still be missed. My focus would be only self-love, not really the love of God at all. As one man said, "If God's love made us central and focused on our value, it would distract us from what is most precious; namely, Himself."[2]

God's love for us should not drive us to higher self-esteem but instead to a higher value of *His* opinion. Ditching the world's measurement ought to be the shove that pushes us into knowing Christ deeply. Our reaction should be something like, "So God loves me and created me with a reason, but what was that reason? How can I know more of Him? How can I please God with my life?"

The question no longer has anything to do with how we look. Now we're looking at God.

AND GOD SAID . . .

What does God value? He doesn't keep it a secret. He spells the answer out pretty clearly.

When God told the prophet Samuel to find a king for Israel, He said, "Do not look on his appearance or on the height of his stature . . . man looks on the outward appearance, but the Lord looks on the heart" (1 Samuel 16:7). For us, this means that while you and I are wonderfully created creatures of God, there are bigger things to worry about than our bodies. It's natural for man to look at the outward appearance, but God's gaze is on what will really matter in the long run. The content of our *hearts* is what God cares about.

So tell me about your guts. Who are you on the inside?

If you weren't reading a book right now, and instead you and I were sitting next to each other on some park bench, I'd ask you about your life story. I'd want you to tell me who you are. What are your plans? What are your gifts? If you're especially frank, I might even dare to ask about your weaknesses. I'd ask how you're broken, and I'd tell you about my fault lines.

Over the past few years in particular, I'd explain, I've become more conscious of my own frailty. I'm a mess. My identity is a tangled knot, with threads of emotions, fears, and doubts pulling me a dozen different directions. I'm afraid of the future most of the time. I've got pride issues, but lately they've been broken a bit by all the falls I've taken.

You and I—we're messes. We'll never be perfect. And although the problems within us are the biggest reasons for the problems outside of us, we usually try to ignore our insides. We think beauty, sex, love, admiration, money, popularity, and whatever else sounds nice at the moment will satisfy us.

We turn back to chasing causes that keep our eyes off the brokenness of ourselves.

God treats the topic differently. He knows satisfaction will be ours only when we let Him fix our brokenness. He dives to the root of the problem, by exposing all the terrible truth of who we are. If He doesn't, we'll never live. We'll never chase the one worthy Cause with all of our being. If He doesn't show us the painful truth, we'll never be free.

WHO WE ARE
(Your Heart Is like a Scary Movie)

It began as an ordinary day in Smalltown, America, when our heroine, Sara, awoke to discover a nightmare.

Birds twittered outside as Sara stumbled out of bed, pulled on some clothes, and sped to the bathroom. She hoped to arrive there before Krissy, her roommate, awoke and demanded they take turns.

Sara grabbed her toothbrush and was about to put it to her teeth when she caught sight of herself in the mirror. The unearthly reflection caused her to blink, and with an ominous clatter, her toothbrush fell to the floor. (Cue the scary music.) Folds of greenish skin wrinkled down her face. (Gasp.) Her eyes, normally a light hazel, had become red bulbs bulging from her sockets. "Aah!" she shrieked.

As her fingers cautiously met the scaly folds of her face, a sensation of pure terror ran through her body. Her face had turned into a Halloween mask overnight. Her long, wavy brown hair had shrunk to only a few spiky strands on her head and a few straggly hairs protruding from her ears. On her arms were pussy white sores that throbbed. It was like a scene out of some twisted horror flick. She was so shocked, Sara couldn't even cry. She simply stared.

A knock sounded at the door. "Sara, let me in! I have class in less than an hour." It was Krissy. Sara froze. There was no way she could be seen like this! Throwing a towel over her head, she opened the door, rushing past Krissy and into her own room.

What was happening? What had she done to cause this . . . this . . . *monster* to take over her body? Was it something she'd eaten the night before? She prayed it wouldn't be permanent, whatever it was.

Then, a terrible, sinking feeling came over her. She knew exactly what was going on. This was no monster. At least, this monster was not something new to who she was. This was her Self. The contents of her heart had spilled over to her body. She had now become on the outside what she had always been on the inside.

All right, I admit it: I'll probably never write a successful screenplay. That story was just too corny.

But I tell the story to bring up this question: What if we had a morning like Sara's? What if we lived in a world where the contents of our heart were clearly visible from the outside? *Would we be beautiful?*

And yet we do live in a world where our insides are shown outwardly. Proverbs 4:23 says that the heart is the "wellspring of life" (NIV). Our lives and our actions all spring from the stuff we allow to grow in our hearts. And is this stuff beautiful?

Not unless you find sewage particularly attractive.

With the amount of arrogance, meanness, lies, and self-satisfaction stored up in my heart, I doubt my image in the mirror would appear any different from Sara's. Our hearts are so sick that they are actually *hostile* to goodness. I can easily identify with the tendency to sin that writer Kris Lundgaard describes:

You can feel the hostility of the flesh whenever you approach God—it makes real love for Him into work:

Digging around the Bible to find a juicy new insight to impress your small group is like sailing the Caribbean, but poring over the Scriptures to find the Lover of your soul is like skiing up Mount Everest. Conjuring up a happy mood with some music you don't even know the words to is like solving 2+2 with a calculator. But savoring the glory of Christ and His tender love until your heart is softened toward Him is like using mental math to calculate pi to the thousandth place.[3]

To many of us, the term "inner beauty" holds little or no meaning. In fact, if you're like me, the phrase makes you groan and roll your eyes. ("Inner beauty? C'mon. Are we on *Sesame Street* or something?") Because the people who judge us on our appearances cannot see our hearts, physical attractiveness is a higher priority. Yet on a scale of 1 to 10, the value of inner beauty would be off the charts. Why? Inside is what God sees.

And what He sees in us isn't pretty.

On the other hand, God's beauty is jaw-dropping. To say that He stands in contrast with our ugliness would be an understatement. Comparing Him to us would be like comparing a rainbow with mud. There is *no* comparison. Christ— who is God in human form—is so inwardly beautiful that we would fall to our knees at a glimpse of His heart.

He doesn't flatter us. Jesus knows exactly how ugly we are. Yet, through Christ's sacrifice, the wickedness that covered us like pussy, oozing sores is forgotten the very moment we repent and place our faith in Him. We become beautiful in the eyes of God. We don't become just sort-of-pretty-but-still-in-need-of-work; we become radiantly stunning. When God looks at us, He sees the glowing purity of His Son.

We may bury our head in shame at all of our faults—but no matter what we do, God sees beauty—a beauty that is not our own but a gift from Him.

Of course, being renamed by Christ does not automatically change us. Although we are forgiven our sins, our habits have yet to be redeemed. Our brokenness has yet to be *fixed*:

> You have heard about Him and were taught in Him . . . to put off your old self, which belongs to your former manner of life and is corrupt through deceitful desires, and to be renewed in the spirit of your minds, and to put on the new self, created after the likeness of God in true righteousness and holiness. (Ephesians 4:21–24)

Change is easier discussed than done. With the bar set so high, it's impossible for us to rewrite our hearts on our own. So what does He do?

Imagine a charcoal-colored heart on an operating table, with spongy holes of decay beneath its membranous sheath. The right atrium oozes pus—a sure sign of infection. Then, a metal scalpel begins scraping. The plaque that blocks each blood vessel is slowly but surely being removed.

That's a picture of you and me. That's our reality. Right now, that's my heart on the operating table. God doesn't ask anything less than a total scraping-clean. It's a painful process we must go through.

To be totally frank, I hate the thought of pain. I don't like that Jesus calls us to this overhauling—and for a long time, I feared what this might mean for me. What will God put me through in this life in order to purify my heart?

When our love for God
abounds more and more,
we begin to change into His image.

It's still not an easy thought, but I'm beginning to understand it a little better. God prunes and reshapes us because He loves us. He knows we will only ever be truly satisfied if our satisfaction is in Him. That's how He's made us. Like a wife who looks for happiness at the spa and with her friends, when her greatest love is waiting for her in her husband, we were made to find our greatest love in Christ. The gunk that takes up our focus keeps us from Him.

Even though I hate the thought of pain, the fear is eclipsed by the fact that, in spite of everything, it's *God* who holds our hearts. Yes, it's a tough operation, but what does the pain matter, knowing that God *Himself* is our surgeon? He doesn't mess up. His scalpel doesn't waver or cause unnecessary agony.

Bibles verses shoot to mind. An Old Testament passage promises, "I will give you a new heart and put a new spirit within you; and I will remove the heart of stone from your flesh and give you a heart of flesh" (Ezekiel 36:26 NASB). Paul writes to a group of believers, "For I am confident of this very thing, that he who began a good work in you will perfect it until the day of Christ Jesus" (Philippians 1:6 NASB).

Inner beauty (or "sanctification") is the name of this heart surgery. Every Jesus-follower must undergo this lifelong procedure. Our hearts are on the operating table, being brought out from the old habits of sin, and our characters are being transformed to give honor to Christ.

True transformation is what Paul emphasized in the last earthly conversation he shared with his Ephesian brothers. By counting himself as nothing, Paul made God his heart's treasure, and this is where sanctification starts. When our love for God abounds more and more, and we count ourselves as less, we automatically begin to change into His image (Philippians 1:9–11). It all starts with that love.

WANDERLUST

Though the enormity of our sin can make us want to throw in the towel—don't even think about giving up!

Although I'm far from the finish line in this race, let me tell you what I've seen.

I've seen God do miracles. I've seen Him prove Himself faithful. I've watched as He's given gifts that are completely undeserved—but He gives them anyway. I've witnessed Him strengthen weary hands and feet so that even after seventy years of running the race, they still have fight left in them.

Since, then, you have been raised with Christ, set your hearts on things above, where Christ is seated at the right hand of God. Set your minds on things above, not on earthly things. For you died, and your life is now hidden with Christ in God.

—COLOSSIANS 3:1–3 NIV

CHAPTER 6

Beauty Killer

There's something timeless, exquisite, and a bit romantic about old houses. I love them. Their vintage architecture—even the fact that their porch swings squeak—makes me want to collapse in a window seat with a book (*Anne of Green Gables*, preferably).

One house in particular has always caught my attention. Recently my friend and I drove by it again, just to gape and dream of one day fixing it up. The poet Keats was right when he wrote that "a thing of beauty is a joy forever."[1] I will forever love that house.

On a quiet cul-de-sac, the abandoned nineteenth-century mansion is hidden behind overgrown grass, vines, and oak trees. It was built as a dream house for the heiress of an oil fortune, and no cost was spared in its construction. My favorite parts of "El Castile" (the house even has a *name*) are its tower and blue stained-glass windows—though they're now covered in vines.

It makes a sad picture to see such a castle fall into disrepair. Every time I drive by, I wish someone would make the house beautiful again.

Honestly, if anyone were to scribble obscene graffiti on the walls of El Castile, I'd feel like beating him up. Whether it's an old house that takes your breath away or a mountain landscape that makes you quiver in your shoes, all of us feel the pull of beauty in some unique way. The destruction of something beautiful should never cease to make our hearts a bit sick. Whether or not it qualifies as actual sin, it certainly feels *wrong* to destroy beauty without reason.

Modesty is the
special combination of
unpretentiousness and *discretion.*

The destruction of the human body should be no exception. It is the greatest masterpiece, the final flourish of God's creativity. There are some serious mountains on this planet, some pretty oceans, coral reefs, and flying fish—but none of these compare to the beauty of you.

I'm not saying this to lift your ego. I'm saying it because it's true. For example, the human mind is an amazing, brilliant thing. Who could imagine that a brain, made up of gray and white matter, could process the taste of pepperoni, let alone dream up the recipe for pizza? (Not that pizza-making is the pinnacle of human achievement, but it's impressive!)

Modesty is a desire not to draw undue attention to oneself, as well as a desire to be wise.

And yet this magnificence is marred constantly. Oscar Wilde once wrote, "No object is so beautiful that, under certain conditions, it will not look ugly." A billion times worse than painting obscenities on the walls of a dream house, we are distracted from the loveliness of womanhood by . . . something we all do and have all done. It's something women do to themselves.

Immodesty.

I'm not building hype around this, to make immodesty sound worse than it is. I think immodesty is gravely important and deserves far more attention than it is usually given.

Because it distracts.

Detracts.

And destroys.

Properly defined, modesty is the special combination of *unpretentiousness* and *discretion*. In other words, it is a desire *not* to draw undue attention to oneself, as well as a desire to be wise. Chew for a minute on what *Webster's 1828* states:

> Modesty springs no less from principle than from feel-ing, and is manifested by retiring, unobtrusive manners . . . and conceding to others all due honor and respect, or even more than they expect or require . . . In females, modesty . . . is used also as synonymous with chastity, or purity of manners. In this sense, modesty results from purity of mind.[2]

That's quite a mouthful, isn't it? To break down the definition, *modesty* is first defined as humility and the respect of others, coming from purity. Often, the word is used to describe clothing. Modest clothing (clothes that show humility, respect, and purity) are clothes that cover more than they reveal.

THE POWER OF THE BODY

Reading a magazine article one day, I was struck by some-thing the author had written: "Advertisers have spent mil-lions learning what makes a person spend time looking at an ad. They've learned that if you really want to stop the reader, use a woman. It seems a photo of a woman will increase the length of time someone spends with an ad by 14–30 percent."[3]

If a *photo* can keep a reader's eyes on the page several seconds longer, how much more power does a real, living, breathing woman have on other people walking down the street? How many eyes does she attract? It's not a sick question, only an honest one. Does a woman's body have the power to draw attention? You bet.

We're joined with
God Himself, with our bodies
as tools to be used for His glory.

While it may feel good at times to take advantage of this power, by using it to turn heads in a room or draw extra attention to ourselves, I'm reminded of the real purpose of the body. When we're saved by Christ, our bodies actually become a part of Him. We're joined with God Himself, with our bodies as tools to be used for His glory. "Do you not know that your bodies are members of Christ?" (1 Corinthians 6:15).

So while our bodies are powerful enough to draw attention, we have a different purpose than baring ourselves for all the world to stare at.

WHEN FASHION GOES TOO FAR

A glance at the clock told Emma that she needed to leave for church soon if she wanted a good seat. She heaved a sigh as she turned around again, inspecting herself in the mirror. The question was about her favorite V-neck shirt. It was red—her best color—but she hadn't worn it since last spring. She was delighted to find it in the back of the closet that morning but disappointed when she tried it on.

Purity is a
struggle for boys, too.

Emma had grown a couple of inches wider since she'd last worn the blouse; although last year it had fit perfectly and was completely modest, this year was different. It retained its flattering color, but the fabric clung to her skin like a wetsuit and revealed her chest. She knew it showed too much.

Just the same, Emma fought with the idea of setting the shirt aside. Practically every woman showed her "headlights" these days. Besides, the top would still be more concealing than most of the outfits displayed on mannequins at the mall. Staring into the mirror, Emma asked herself aloud, "Why not?"

Modesty is never simply an option. The Bible gives us little room for doubt on that note: "Women should adorn themselves in respectable apparel, with modesty and self-control" (1 Timothy 2:9). If we want to obey God, we have to acknowledge that verse. We should be willing enough to comply just because *it's there*.

However, there is a *clear* reason for this command: Girls aren't the only ones who shed tears and scribble frustrated journal entries over their wayward hearts. Purity is a struggle for the boys, too. Though where we fight the thickest of the battle in our emotions, guys must fight their eyes most. Men are sexually aroused by sight.

Provocative clothing does just what the word suggests—it provokes sexual temptation and lust. If a woman wears a revealing top or ultratight pants, she is opening herself up for public viewing and becoming a walking advertisement for sex. It's not a pretty thought—and probably not the image she meant to achieve when she picked her wardrobe. She may have thought she was simply following a trend. But to a man who sees her, her clothing (or lack of it) is an invitation. The sight of her brings to mind thoughts from the gutter.

A guy explained the experience like this: "When I see that girl in the short skirt, and I want to stare at her legs . . . I have to force myself to look away. Physically wrench my head to look [in] the other direction, because if I don't, my eyes are going right back. . . . I'll think about cars, math, sports—whatever it takes to get my thoughts off that body."[4]

Another man wrote of his inward "antenna" for women: "I have had to literally retrain my sense, to turn down the strength of my antenna when it comes to noticing women in public. When the signal comes to my brain now, telling me that a woman is in my vicinity, I make a conscious attempt not to respond to the signal, but instead to look directly ahead."[5]

Guys don't often discuss their visual temptation with girls for obvious reasons. Lust is an awkward topic. I don't know anyone who enjoys talking about it, but you wouldn't believe how many wives and mothers I have personally heard advocate modesty after finding out from their husbands and sons the effect immodesty has on their minds. Although it isn't a popular subject to discuss over the dinner table, the results of immodesty are real.

The matter may seem of little importance to us—we may think that only women with a certain body type are tempting to men—and that surely *we* are not among them. But according to the Modesty Survey, taken by more than 1,600 Christian guys, over 96 percent of men and boys surveyed agreed that "modesty is important for all girls, regardless of height, weight, build, etc." And it's not just old men or young guys who struggle with immodest images. A boy commented, "An ugly girl, [and] a short girl, [and] a model can all dress immodestly. And regardless [of body type], they are a stumbling block to us."[6] (Keep in mind, that's from a *twelve*-year-old.)

But why does it matter to us what goes on in a guy's mind? It's sickening, even disturbing, and realizing that lust happens may make us suspicious of guys for a while, but what does it have to do with *us*? It's *his* problem. It's his decision to sin, *right*?

Yet the Bible makes clear our responsibility to help *protect* each other as brothers and sisters in Christ from temptation; we're not supposed to throw each other to the wolves. We're family. We don't live for ourselves alone. Anything that can paralyze a brother or sister from chasing harder after Christ should be concerning to us *all* (1 Corinthians 8:9).

It must be common for Christian guys to be bombarded with images while out in public, but it's convicting for me to wonder whether guys are bombarded when around *Christian* girls. When guys are at church or in the company of friends, are they *encouraged* or *discouraged* to stay pure by the clothing of the women around them? How can guys be expected to stand strong against temptation when those Christian sisters, who ought to be their allies, surround them with thighs and midriffs?

Even when we share concern for our brothers, when that shirt hangs just a little *too* well on us or that pair of jeans hugs our hips so tightly we find it difficult to bend down, it's easy to begin rationalizing. We think that compared to others, we're still modest. It isn't a big deal. Selfishness takes over, and the question of whether it's right fades into oblivion. When we're not sure if an article of clothing completely fits the 1 Timothy 2:9 category or not, we push the question to the back of our minds and wear it anyway.

I know the steps of rationalizing because I've walked through them myself, more often than I feel comfortable admitting. Why do we do this?

MODESTY AND THE GOSPEL

Maybe we've forgotten the reason for clothes in the first place. I like the question Mary Kassian poses in her rich, wise book *Girls Gone Wise*: "Why does nakedness normally cause shame?" She quotes Genesis, where Adam and Eve gave in to sin and then immediately felt the need to get some clothes on.

Nakedness was natural and fitting for Adam and Eve when they were pure and innocent. But when that purity and innocence was lost, they became painfully embarrassed by their naked condition. Why? What's the connection between sin and nakedness? . . . . Eve's sin was self-exaltation. She arrogantly refused to acknowledge that God alone was God. When she took the fruit, she defied who He was and made herself out to be something that she was not. After she sinned, Eve's eyes opened to the fact that she was not the goddess she had presumptuously made herself out to be . . . . For the first time ever . . . she tried to conceal the gap between what she was and what she should have been by covering her most intimate, vulnerable parts with leaves . . . [but] nothing could hide the dishonor, disgrace, and embarrassment of their rebellion against their Creator.

God did what Adam and Eve were unable to do. He covered them and made them presentable. He shed the

blood of an animal—probably a lamb—and clothed
them with its skin. By means of a bloody sacrifice, He
covered their sin and shame. Do you see the symbolism
here? . . . . Clothing bears witness to the fact that we have
lost the glory and beauty of our original sin-free selves.
It confesses that we need a covering—His covering—
to atone for our sin and alleviate our shame. It testifies
to the fact that God solved the problem of shame permanently and decisively with the blood of His own Son.
. . . Clothing is an outward, visible symbol of an inward,
spiritual reality. When you "put on Christ," He covers
your shame and makes you what you should be.[7]

Hearing the purpose of clothing helps me put modesty
in perspective. It means that we don't have to look specifically
for frumpy clothing in order to be modest or that we don't
need to adopt legalist rules in our approach to modesty.

For me, the problem has little to do with knowing
what is modest and what isn't. The Holy Spirit often lets
me know that; I *know* when I'm wearing something I
shouldn't. My problem is with submission. I don't *like* submitting to God all the time.

Why do we struggle with submitting so much? When
we know that our clothes are a reflection of Christ and the
gospel, and when we know modesty is important, why
does disregarding the Spirit feel so attractive? Why is sin
enticing?

Because we haven't spent enough time remembering.

Every time I look with one eye on the Cross and another on my own sin, I run out of words trying to describe the wonder of Christ's sacrifice for me. The realization that my sins are no more, because of His *blood*, is staggering. I'm so undeserving—and God is so merciful.

It's like waking up from a dream that feels like reality, only to collide face-first with genuine, blazing life. I constantly need a reminder that those nails that dug into His nerves were mine. They were *meant* to be mine, but God took them instead. Exquisite pain paid for the sins I commit, have committed, and will commit. How can I move on from this?

Pastor C. J. Mahaney wrote in *Living the Cross-Centered Life*:

> If there's anything in life that we should be passionate about, it's the gospel. And I don't mean passionate only about sharing it with others. I mean passionate in thinking about it, dwelling on it, rejoicing in it, allowing it to color the way we look at the world. Only one thing can be of first importance to each of us. And only the gospel ought to be.[8]

Unfortunately, we don't often let the Cross shape our thinking. We don't stare at it long enough. When the question of modesty comes up, we toss reservation in the trash. We forget the cost of sin. We forget how serious our offenses are to a holy God. By moving on from the Cross, we belittle the opinion of God. We let the world gain a foothold in our lives.

Emma's predicament over her favorite red V-neck has been my own many times over, but that does not lessen the seriousness of it. Just as every other area of our lives, modesty needs to be brought under the dominion of Christ. And when we're fighting to surrender, it helps to remember the Cross.

PRACTICALLY SPEAKING:
FOUR REASONS FOR MODESTY

Let's say you disagree with my take on modesty completely. You find it revolting. This issue is one you really, really fight with. Or maybe you're the debater type (I love you guys), and you want some more points. That's great. We have a faith that holds up well under the weight of logic. While our faith isn't based on logic, we still needn't run away from intellectual reasoning. Our faith was invented by God, who formed us in His image, creating us logical and sentient, like Himself. Faith can't be entirely summed up in rationale (there's a beauty that can't be summarized by logic), but reasoning can definitely be used to support our faith. After all, we're not only called to love God with hearts but with our minds as well. So, if those Kassian or Mahaney quotes weren't sufficient, let's take a look at how logic points to modesty.

CHOOSE MODESTY.
IT LASTS LONGER.

So swallowing your conscience, you chose to wear the top that sticks just a teensy bit too close to your curves. The day is over. The top is in the laundry. What did you gain? When I've stubbornly worn something in spite of the nagging feeling that it was immodest, at the end of the day, I haven't been one bit better off than if I had worn something else. In fact, I'm worse off, because now I'm awash with conviction over thumbing my nose at the Holy Spirit.

In other words, disobedience doesn't pay. While the pleasure may last for a moment when we receive some desired attention or like how the clothes accentuate us, that moment is fleeting.

DID ANYONE CARE?

I remember reading somewhere the words of a wise woman who reported that her husband advised her not to fuss over the approval of people. He told her, "Don't worry about what others think, because, honestly, they don't think about you."

This is true, and slightly embarrassing. How often have I fretted over the opinion of someone else, when I probably barely register on his or her radar?

Is there more
to you than meets the eye?

How long do you think others will be impressed by a particularly attractive, immodest set of clothes? Will they remember how good your body looked next month, or next week, or even tomorrow? Not likely—unless it's the kind of lustful image you don't want sticking in someone's mind. So what exactly is the benefit of dressing against our consciences, anyway? It's hard to find any benefit.

GRAB YOUR STETHOSCOPE

If choosing the modest outfit was a really, really, really tough decision, you may want to stop and think. Grab your stethoscope and conduct a heart check. What made doing the right thing so difficult? Perhaps it was hard because you were waging yet another battle with your flesh's natural desire to sin. But maybe immodest dressing is a sin that has been secretly sneaking into your mind for a while now. Have you been harboring a need to be noticed?

Consider this: Have you been reminded recently of God's love for you as shown in the gospel, and meditated on that love? Or have your thoughts been occupied with other inferior loves (guys, the approval of friends based on your appearance, etc.)? Have you reminded yourself that the reason you're even alive is to glorify your Maker, and nothing (including clothes) should stand in the way of His being glorified?

Please don't take this as me pointing fingers. I'm not trying to diagnose the heart problems of others. I'm only speaking of what I've learned from my own.

IS THERE MORE TO YOU
THAN MEETS THE EYE?

Modesty says yes to this question. It shows there's a deeper fiber in the girl than a yearning for attention, and more individuality than a need to accept each and every trend that bares itself on the runway. Modesty reflects that there are higher things than vanity on the priority list of the wearer. It suggests you're not guy crazy.

And a lack of modesty reveals, well, more than just skin. It's indicative of our priorities. That is not to deny that some girls are simply immodest because they don't know any better or because they're naïve and haven't ever thought through their clothing choices, but to those who *know* what is right and do otherwise—that's sin (according to James 4:17). And sin doesn't start suddenly; it grows as an outshoot of our choices and thought life.

So is there more to me than meets the eye of those who see me? Is there more to you? What do my clothes communicate to others? And what about God? What am I saying to *Him*?

These are questions for the heart.[9]

Womanhood is a call

. . . The strength to answer this call is given us as we look up toward the Love that created us, remembering that it was that Love that first . . . made us at the very beginning real men and real women. As we conform to that Love's demands we shall become more humble, more dependent— on Him and on one another—and even (dare I say it?) more splendid.

—ELISABETH ELLIOT, *Let Me Be a Woman*

CHAPTER 7

Finding
Femininity

At one time, a very average little girl lived on a very average little street in an average little town in the United States. We will call her "Jane." Jane was born with talents, strengths, and weaknesses, like other children. However, unlike other children, Jane had no parents.

It's not that they never existed. She had them at one time. But the day she decided she didn't like their rules or the broccoli her mother served at dinner, Jane quit the family. She wanted to decide for herself who she would be.

Jane decided to treat her friends the same way. Although with her talents and personality, Jane managed to make friends, she rarely was asked to play hide-and-seek or jump rope because she'd never adhere to the rules. She preferred to make her own.

Years passed and Jane grew. When she was a woman, she was very much the same as when she was a child (except a bigger version). While as a child her main rebellion concerned broccoli, as an adult Jane revolted at the idea of abiding by the laws set by God. Jane wanted to decide for herself, as always. The older she grew, the more headstrong and demanding she became.

One day, as Jane sat in church, she heard the pastor speak of God having different, specific designs for men and women. She learned that God had created her with a certain purpose in His mind. This angered Jane. It was yet another set of rules she'd have to dodge. Jane ditched church and decided that if the Bible contained such restrictive rules for women, it must not be true.

This was the way Jane lived every moment of her life. She never married when she fell in love, because she knew marriage involved submission (more rules). When she was pregnant, she had an abortion because she refused to be chained to motherhood (more rules).

Finally, one day, she found that she wasn't happy to be female. So Jane forgot she was, which was actually what she was trying to do all along.

TRUE STORY

Jane's story sounds like some twisted children's storybook. There's something eerie about the story of a little girl who doesn't want to be a little girl. By living in rebellion, Jane lived in denial of her true identity as a creation of God—and that makes her life a very sad story.

Worse yet, Jane's story is true. Her journey symbolizes the evolution of the feminist movement throughout the years.

FEMINISM AS A CAUSE

You may be saying, "Wait a sec. I thought this book was about causes that get in the way of the worthwhile Cause. Why am I reading about feminism all of a sudden?"

On the surface, we might not think feminism is one of our distracting, little "c" causes. Compared to an issue like beauty, it's not commonplace. You don't see girls tripping over each other to see who can be the "most feminist."

Why, then, am I talking about it here?

While we may not think feminism is a cause that can keep us from giving Christ total worship, the *concepts* promoted by feminist teachings often *do* get in the way. Here, what trips us up isn't so much identifying with a movement but adopting some of the movement's ideas.

What are the feminist ideas I find so expressly unbiblical? I'll get to that in a moment. Before we jump in completely, we both should probably remind ourselves of what feminism originally aimed to accomplish.

THE CORE OF A MOVEMENT

Feminism began as a group of ideas held by only a handful of women. The ideology spread rapidly, forming the modern feminist movement that touches the lives of women *and* men in countless ways today. What has caused the rabid divorce rate, daily abortions, and widespread acceptance of homosexuality?[1] Our sin nature, for certain—but feminism surely has had a hand in the process.

Feminist philosophy
has irrevocably changed
our minds about womanhood.
I like the idea of women being brave,
intelligent, and strong-willed.

Feminism claims to have rescued women from lives of servitude to men. While it's unlikely that most modern feminists would assert that feminism was simply a fight for equal pay and equal rights, the philosophy itself has extended far beyond laws and activism.

Feminist philosophy has irrevocably changed our minds about womanhood. Supposedly, it has brought women freedom, liberation. Yet I believe that feminism has brought the opposite.

Instead of liberation, women have met a level of confusion that previous generations never knew. Feminism has stolen from women the knowledge of our identities. We have no answers to questions such as, "Who am I?" and

"Why was I made this way?" We don't really understand that other variations of womanhood exist outside of the feminist model. We aren't free. Thanks to the "Women's Liberation Movement," women have lost nearly all sense of who they are.

If truth is to be found, feminism's pretty face must be torn away. Feminism must be unmasked as the thief that it is. I have a hunch that when we tear away the ideas that have infiltrated our world for so long, we'll discover something precious: ourselves.

PRETTY FACE

I'm not going to lie, there's an element to feminism I find attractive. I like the idea of women being brave, intelligent, and strong-willed. I tend to get really pumped in the "girl power" movies when the Kelly Clarkson song comes on in the background, and the heroine finally makes her victory speech to Harvard or explodes into a string of karate moves. Part of that, I think, comes from a good foundation; girls *can* be brave, intelligent, and strong-willed (but only if that will is tempered by reasonableness, which submits to the will of God. Ha, you knew there'd be a clause).

But just because an idea is attractive at first glance doesn't mean it's good. Although feminism tries to use strong, independent-thinking, smart women as its spokespeople, there's a lot more to feminism than those elements.

And even though feminists may claim to have a corner on "strong, independent-thinking, smart women," those actually existed prefeminism. The Bible actually has a few listed in its pages. Thinking women aren't a new phenomenon by any means.

So what is feminism anyway?

Ani Difranco, a singer/songwriter and feminist, once said, "My idea of feminism is self-determination, and it's very open-ended: every woman has the right to become herself, and do whatever she needs to do."[2] That sounds all right, doesn't it? What's wrong with self-determination? The right to become myself sounds nice. Welcome to the pretty face of feminism.

To find the truth
of our identities, ultimately, we must not look to ourselves. We must head for the source of all truth.

Before *approving* "self-determination," we must define it. The feminist movement has been a cheerleader for "naming oneself." Essentially this is the same as saying, "You have the right to become whatever you wish to become, regardless what anyone (especially God) says. Look inside yourself to find who you are."

But I wonder, if a girl already does not know who she is, how can she discover it by looking to *herself*? Won't she be more puzzled than ever?

Here lies the problem and danger of feminism. Instead of basing its view of manhood and womanhood on God's Word, feminism based its view on what a woman *feels* about who she is. She has the role of figuring out for herself exactly what she was created to do. And there's the recipe for disaster.

I'm reminded of the two girls George MacDonald wrote about who were guided by their own constantly changing emotions: "They had a feeling, or a feeling had them, till another feeling came and took its place. When a feeling was there, they felt as if it would never go; when it was gone they felt as if it had never been; when it returned, they felt as if it had never gone." Confusing, isn't it? And that's the whole point. Looking to ourselves for answers ends only in confusion.

How can we determine *ourselves* who we are? I've spent hours of my life devoted to introspection, as I imagine you have, too. We all want to know who we are, why we're here, and what makes us tick. That introspection is necessary, but with so much time devoted to "interpreting ourselves," we can easily lose sight of the fact that only God can know us completely. To find the truth of our identities, ultimately, we must not look to ourselves. We must head for the source of all truth.

If I wanted to learn how a cell phone is assembled, it

would make sense to ask someone who assembles cell phones. To discover how to build a piano, I should probably ask a piano builder. In the same way, it only makes sense to go to the Creator of women to find who we were meant to be. God alone knows how He built us. Every aspect of our natures—from the reason why certain people especially love football to why some possess an innate gift of organization—is known by God because it's all in *His* design. Why should we ask anyone else's advice?

Yet here's where feminism gets so dicey, and this is what makes me approach it with caution: looking to the *Bible* to find who we are is incompatible with feminism too. It's impossible to become what *I* imagine a woman should be like while taking seriously what God has already determined. Feminist Phyllis Trible wrote, "If no man can serve two masters, no woman can serve two authorities, a master called Scripture and a mistress called feminism."[3] Likewise, Annie Laurie Gaylor wrote, "Let's forget about the *mythical* Jesus and look for encouragement, solace, and inspiration from real women. . . . Two thousand years of patriarchal rule under the shadow of the cross ought to be enough to turn women toward the feminist 'salvation' of this world."[4]

Clearly, there is an anti-God sentiment expressed by this core "just believe in yourself" message of feminism. After all, how can I believe in God and myself at the same time? A choice must be made between the two. Unfortunately, because the very basis of feminism is to invent for ourselves our identity without God's input, God often is shoved out of the picture. Feminism is all about me.

THE MYTH OF EQUALITY

"But didn't the feminist movement bring about a lot of good things? Wasn't the whole point to promote equality between men and women?" This is true—though not completely. Feminists proudly claim to be the champions of the idea of equality. Many feminists have said that they believe men and women are equal, *but they were not the first.*

When we read our Bibles closely, the truth is obvious. *God* was the first to proclaim the equal value of men and women, thousands of years before feminism existed. Men are no more precious than women, and women are no more precious than men. All human life is of immense worth to God.

From the very start of the Bible, it is emphasized that God made both male and female in His image. Genesis 1:27 says, "So God created man in his own image, in the image of God he created him; male and female he created them." Both, while different from each other and made different by God, are held as equally valuable. Both are His precious creation. As it says in 1 Corinthians 11:11–12, "Nevertheless, in the Lord woman is not independent of man nor man of woman; for as woman was made from man, so man is now born of woman. And all things are from God."

All things are from God.

While around the world, in many different cultures, women are horrifically abused simply because of their gender, no such oppression is permitted in God's kingdom. He grants us fundamental equality and calls us to respect each other as fellow bearers of the *imago dei*—the image of God.

Although feminists declare equality between men and women, it is not uncommon for men to be unequally bashed. Radical feminist Andrea Dworkin said, "I want to see a man beaten to a bloody pulp with a high-heel shoved in his mouth, like an apple in the mouth of a pig."[5] Sally Gearhart proposed, "The proportion of men must be reduced to and maintained at approximately 10 percent of the human race."[6]

This is not to say that if you've ever associated yourself with the feminist movement, you hold these beliefs. You probably don't. (I don't know of *anyone* who does.) But those quotes are revealing of where feminism can lead. Pro-feminism can become anti-men. Does that sound like equality to you?

If you're like me, that information doesn't help much— and it's more than a little depressing. Why? Because, basically, I've just argued against the only option our culture hands us as girls. If we want to be brave, visionary women, we're told to be feminists. That's it. If we choose any other options, we're told we're being "weak minded" and "visionless."

Fear not. Your choice is not between "feminist diva" or

"Victorian housewife whose worth is only ornamental." Those aren't your only options. God has made another way.

GOD'S BIG IDEA

A wife of noble character, who can find? Martha Stewart has nothing on her; neither does Wonder Woman. Her husband can trust confidently in her wisdom. Whatever she does, she does for the best interest of her family.

Before the sun has risen above the horizon, every morning she awakes early to cook breakfast and prepare for the rest of the day. Selfish ambition isn't found anywhere on her radar, but she owns wit by the bucketful.

She buys her family's clothes shrewdly—finding the best product for her money. With her "spare" time, she investigates ventures that will help provide for her family. Her hard-earned money is invested in a plot of land in which she plans to start a vineyard.

Working devotedly into the night, she keeps at her task until certain to bring profit to her family. She prefers clothing of a fine quality and decorates her home with as much beauty as she can bring it, making bedcoverings and clothing herself. On top of it all, she sews clothes and sells them to a local store.

However business-smart she is, her hands never neglect to reach out to the poor. Her heart is one of compassion and devotion to her family. To them, she is a voice of wisdom and integrity. Her children look to her gratefully, blessing her. Her husband praises her with the highest praise he can bestow: "Many women do noble things, but you surpass them all."

This is the standard God has set. Contrary to many understandings of womanhood, the model of womanhood found in Proverbs 31 is quite complex, challenging, and amazingly—free.

FREE INDEED

So maybe your heart didn't jump for joy when you read the description of the Proverbs 31 woman. Keeping a home isn't high on the list of glamorous occupations. Feminism has so infiltrated our culture that it has wiped out nearly every positive image of homemaking. Even Bible-believing Christians can have a tough time grappling with the idea that Christian women have a designated role in the care of the home.

A woman once wrote me to say that she does not believe all women are meant to share the role that the Proverbs 31 woman portrayed. She explained (rather snottily) that she had talents outside of homemaking and did not intend to "waste her mind on cleaning toilets and changing diapers."

What a tragic perspective. To think that the job of the Proverbs 31 woman was brainless would be like calling Chuck Norris a wimp. It just doesn't work. Operating as the manager of her household, this amazing woman was challenged to use every single talent in her possession. Creativity was required. Logic and analytical skills were invaluable. I can't imagine doing her job half so well, and I don't think anyone who realized the extent of her work could consider it demeaning of womanhood.

It's also interesting to note that the Proverbs 31 woman was clearly not kept at home every moment. She sold clothing and planted a vineyard. (She worked!) Much of her activity took place outside her house. But a clear distinction must be made between this lady and the "career woman" image our culture has so firmly placed in our minds: the Proverbs 31 woman used her talents for a higher purpose than personal acclaim. She didn't expect her work would buy her a closet of Gucci bags or bring invitations to black-tie parties. All of her endeavors ended with the goal of serving. By nurturing her home, raising godly children, and honoring her husband, she brought glory to God. That was her ambition.

While the Proverbs 31 woman was certainly not too proud to care for her children and surely loved them enough to ensure their toilets were clean (even if it meant she had to scrub them herself), she was not chained down by her role. She reveled in it. It was her element. Proverbs 14:1 says that it is a *wise* woman who builds her house, but a foolish woman tears her house apart by her own actions.

Much like a lighthouse, the biblical woman stands as a beacon to others, signaling the love of Christ and obedience to Him. She has a noble calling that often takes place in the home, where women find their greatest power and influence.

"BUT ISN'T THIS LIKE, BONDAGE?"

I'm not trying to preach or rant at you; I'm just a young person trying to figure out what God wants for me. I don't have "special insight." This stuff I'm talking about isn't something I claim to have down or to understand completely. And I'm not saying that my interpretation of these principles is entirely right. All I know is that a biblical basis for women's roles can't be denied.

The Bible gives us a pretty clear outline, which I'll try to overview briefly. Women are told to:

- ◆ Love the Lord with all their hearts, taking advantage of the time that they're unmarried (1 Corinthians 7:34)

- ◆ Be pure (Proverbs 7) and modest, taking guidance from older, godly women (Titus 2:3–4)

- ◆ Be keepers at home (Proverbs 31:10–31)

- ◆ Submit to, respect, and support their husbands; (Ephesians 5:22–33) Unmarried women are to submit to their parents.

- ◆ Not teach/have authority over men in spiritual matters (1 Corinthians 11:1–16)

In the grand scheme of things, there are relatively few verses in the Bible on gender roles, or the different actions men and women should take. (If you have not already, I highly recommend reading through the verses listed above.) The reason why these rules are so relatively few, I believe, is because God didn't create rules regarding gender roles to give us a prison.

Those rules exist so that we might glorify God as much as possible. I think we'll find that when we humble our hearts before Him, truly seeking His will, that gender roles are blessings more than oppressive policies. When making rules for manhood and womanhood, God did not create molds and try to stuff men and women into them; He *designed* us to fit. We aren't imprisoned by the Proverbs 31 woman because God created us to fill those shoes.

I like this description from the book *Recovering Biblical Manhood and Womanhood*:

Two women may jump from an airplane and experience the thrilling freedom of free-falling. But there is a difference: one is encumbered by a parachute on her back and the other is free from this burden. Which person is most free? The one without the parachute feels free— even freer, since she does not feel the constraints of the parachute straps. But she is not truly free. She is in bondage to the force of gravity and to the deception that all is well because she feels unencumbered. . . . That is the way many women (and men) today think of freedom. They judge it on the basis of immediate sensations of unrestrained license or independence. . . . But the mature and wise woman does not seek this freedom by bending reality to fit her desires. She seeks it by being transformed in the renewal of her desires to fit in with God's perfect will (Romans 12:2). *The greatest freedom is found in being so changed by God's Spirit that you can do what you love to do and know that it conforms to the design of God and leads to life and glory.*[7]

In other words, the woman who thinks she is most free will realize the hard truth when she hits the ground, but the woman who puts *on* the parachute is free to *enjoy* the ride, knowing that in the end she won't, well, die.

I have a sneaking suspicion that when we do embrace femininity with a mind open to God's will, asking, "How do I fit here? What is it You want to do in my life?" we'll see His commands in Scripture as they really are: loving laws to help us live in the most satisfying way—not to pull us back but to set us on the trail to true freedom.

CORNER PILLARS

Out of the spotlight as this job may seem, working in the home is a pivotal part of a woman's calling. The strength of families (and ultimately the strength of nations) rests considerably upon the faithful service of us girls. Psalm 144:12 speaks of daughters being "like corner pillars, cut for the structure of a palace." Corner pillars are not only towers of beauty; they are the support of the structure.

Although young or unmarried women may not share the same responsibilities that a married woman possesses, they equally share the responsibility to glorify God in whatever circumstances He's placed them. An unmarried woman can support her parents and help nurture younger siblings in walking with Christ. Away from her parents and immediate family, she can serve and use her God-given gifts in the context of the church. She can reach out to younger girls through friendship and by example.

If you think about it, this call for us to be involved in community is exactly what we need. Just consider how many of your female friends—whether introverts or extroverts—need and desire deep relationships. We long for community *because we were made for it.* God's command for us to interact in community isn't a contradiction to who we are—it's a complement to it. What's more, it's in community that we can have a huge influence on the world.

When French sociologist Alexis de Tocqueville visited the United States during the 1800s, he was shocked to see how women were treated. Unlike the popular attitude in Europe, American women by and large loved the home. What's more, they made it a peaceful refuge for their families. What was the consequence of this difference?

As for myself, I do not hesitate to avow that although the women of the United States are confined within the narrow circle of domestic life, and their situation is in some respects one of extreme dependence, I have nowhere seen women occupying a loftier position; and if I were asked, now that I am drawing to the close of this work, in which I have spoken of so many important things done by the Americans, to what the singular prosperity and growing strength of that people ought mainly to be attributed, I should reply: To the superiority of their women.[8]

This truth is not unique to America. I would venture to say that *any* nation with wives and daughters who are fervently involved in their families will be a stronger nation, simply because its families are stronger.

Knowing this, how can anyone honestly say that femininity is pointless, weak, or insignificant? There is a power and beauty in womanhood as God planned it that no worldly formula could rival. We have been given the tasks of loving and serving. Is this drudgery? Sometimes. But is it unimportant? No, not ever. Not when we are the strength of a kingdom.

We have in our hands a choice. It's worth measuring out cautiously; the options deserve to be weighed with care. If you're a follower of Jesus, you've been chosen by God to be one of His people; if you're female, you've been called to femininity.

While we may need time to dig into Scripture to understand exactly how femininity will play itself out in our lives, we do have a question to ask. Will we take seriously this charge from God? It's all too easy to push this question to the back of our minds. Will we force ourselves to wrestle it out? Argue about the details of femininity later; it boils down to accepting or denying the call of God.

Will I submit to follow, whatever this calling may mean for me?

APPLYING IT: LOVE THE HOME

Picture a girl who daydreams about the future when she'll become a lawyer/journalist/politician/linguist/nurse, etc., and scoffs at the idea of homemaking. Do you think in ten years, when she's married with kids, she'll be content at home?

Of course not. I've met girls fitting that description— dear, sweet, smart, young Christians who want marriage some faraway day, but are quick to declare that they have "more to do with their lives" than marriage or becoming a mother. Their dreams are exclusively career-oriented, and they'd rather jump off a bridge than admit that the home carries any attraction for them.

Mark my words: I don't think that *everyone* can, will, or should get married right out of high school. I don't think marriage is the chief purpose of a woman (though the family *may* be one of God's tools in her life for bringing Him glory). I think these girls have it right in saying that there's more to life than marriage.

What I find scary and a bit sad is often the *attitude* behind the words. The unspoken idea is distaste—dare I say even a *fear*—of the home. As if these women will somehow lose their identities if they—heaven forbid!—marry and find themselves cooking dinner during the evening. I think often the fear is that they will become like some other women they see, women they perceive to be caged by a home life of boredom. This attitude is not the exclusive property of "some girls." I sat down to talk this over with my friend Hännah Schlaudt.

Hännah is a homeschool graduate from Richmond, Virginia. She recently insisted that the next time we meet, we have a cookie-baking contest. To be honest, I'm a little nervous. I'm not sure I want to match my cookie-baking skills against an oldest daughter of a family of nine kids. My bet is that she's made a fair share of cookies in her time. Here, Hännah fits the stereotype of a happy little home-making homeschooler.

The only way to shake ourselves free from our home phobia is to learn to love the home.

During the semester, however, Hännah lives on campus at a well-known Christian university, where she is currently double-majoring in English and Christian thought. In between keeping up with her rigorous academic schedule, she noticed the tendency of her friends either to mock the home or feel ashamed of spending time outside of it.

When I asked why she thought it was common for girls to shy away from the home, she replied, "Well, if they're even a bit ambitious, they'll feel guilty about wasting talent. And maybe they just want to prove they're as smart as the next girl (or smarter), and having 'being a mom' as their ambition does not sound like a goal of a 'smart girl' but rather a low-achiever who maybe wasn't that great at algebra."

Hännah noticed these feelings were popular with female high school seniors: "I've seen it a lot more. [Fear] may even be their reason for going to college—they don't want to face marriage as an option for a while yet, because they're afraid of or not interested in it. Honest-to-goodness quotes from those girls have been things like, 'I just don't want to have to bother with children. They're such a handful,' and 'Why should I waste my brain like that?' "

Ouch. The feelings Hännah reported sounded uncomfortably familiar. While I can't deny that sometimes when I'm cooking dinner or reorganizing a room to make it more attractive, something inside my heart thuds with exuberance over a job well done—why is it that I'm full of awkwardness when I admit I'm as happy at home as I am anywhere else (and happier, usually)? Where does this embarrassment come from?

I don't know why we can feel this way. Maybe it has something to do with pride. Maybe it has something to do with feminism messing with our heads. I only know a part of the answer—we must lose our wrong thinking about the home. And the only way to shake ourselves free from our home phobia is to learn to love it—not just resign ourselves to the fact that we'll probably spend a bit of time in the home during the course of our lives, but to look at the home and the homemaker with respect.

I'm not trying to overemphasize the home here. I realize that it is just one facet (albeit a very important one) of femininity. Being a girl isn't *just* about living at home, and that's not your only form of influence. I'm talking about it at such length because, to a degree, I'm trying to get it straight in my own head.

I've found so much *emptiness* in my perspective when it comes to this specific part of my feminine calling. I've grown up (maybe like you) hearing so much about other areas of my life—career, talents, humanitarian work—where I can make an impact, while hearing almost nothing proportionally about women in the home. When the topic was mentioned, the "home" was made to sound separate, like a calling that must be pursued exclusively and never alongside other areas of life. I felt as if I were being served an ultimatum: "You can either interact with the world *or* seclude yourself in a convent . . . er . . . I mean, home."

So that being said, I want to plead with you—whether you pursue a degree or stay in your kitchen and learn to bake—to realize that the home is not a place to scoff at. Don't let visions of dirty dishes, laundry, dusting, and vacuuming cloud your vision. The home is a sanctuary, a safe place where a family can be its true self. Home is a place femininity was created to love.

Femininity for
young women is simply learning to live in the wisdom of God.

I love what Dorothy Patterson said, as quoted in the book *Feminine Appeal*: "Homemaking—being a full-time wife and mother—is not a destructive drought of uselessness but an overflowing oasis of opportunity; it is not a dreary cell to contain one's talents and skills but a brilliant catalyst to channel creativity and energies into meaningful work."[9]

This is said to bring you hope. Caring for the home won't destroy your individuality. Practicing disciplines like housecleaning, cooking, etc., are the "nuts and bolts" of homemaking—they're necessary skills that free you up/enable you to use your other talents.

FEMININE AT FIFTEEN

Growing up, it always seemed to me that femininity is something primarily for older women—you know, in their thirties and forties, with families and children. I began to wonder if there was a kind of biblical femininity that really applied to me as a, say, fourteen-, fifteen-, or sixteen-year-old girl.

I'm starting to suspect that femininity for a teenager is not about wearing skirts and "looking feminine" or the stereotypes of butter-churning and chicken raising (though I personally love butter-churning, I'm not so fond of chickens). Femininity for young women is simply learning to live in the wisdom of God. It means learning to be set apart, not in the sense of a nun or pioneer woman off in the woods, but having a heart that is set apart.

Biblical femininity means caring more about being like a "wise woman" of the Bible than the women set forth by *Vogue*. That, of course, is tougher than it looks on the surface. When everybody says life's about seducing guys, looking out for yourself, and making friends with the "hot, naughty, and important," it's tough to have a heart that just wants to sit at Jesus' feet. The world will say (I guarantee, it'll happen) that you are invalid if you don't follow its agenda. The world will say you're prudish if you bow out of something because it threatens to suck your attention away from eternity. The world will tell you to disobey your parents because it's the "normal" thing to do. You'll hear that it's okay to be led totally by emotions and to throw wisdom and patience out the window. The world doesn't understand what it means to obey the voice of the Spirit.

Standing up against those lies—that's what it means to be truly, biblically feminine. Yeah, it's the same calling

Christian guys receive, but you're going to face different temptations and you're going to have different weaknesses. You're going to have to work to submit your girlish heart— probably including your tendencies toward emotionalism, toward fantasizing and worrying about the future, your overconcern with beauty—to God's teachings. That's not a job for cowards.[10]

MEET KRISTIN: AN AMERICAN GIRL

My friend Kristin Personius had one such dilemma once she graduated from high school. She wanted to obey God, but there were so many voices giving her conflicting advice, she didn't know what to do.

You can probably understand her problem. It seemed like everyone and their next-door neighbor were asking, "Do you have any plans for college?" "Have you decided on a major?" "Are you moving out of state?" Kristin was expected to come up with a plan for the rest of her life.

The problem was, Kristin had grown up with many Christian friends who had differing views of college. Some believed girls should never, ever pursue degrees. Some believed that if she didn't go to college, she'd be making one of the biggest mistakes of her life. Kristin felt pulled in both directions.

"Ah, the world does confuse me," Kristin vented to me in an email. "I have to live with the questions, the unspoken condemnation, the nagging misunderstanding of people I know and some that I love." I understood Kristin's dilemma because God often uses our friends to advise us in their wisdom. If they disagree with our pursuits, we probably should think twice. Yet all the while, we should compare their advice to God's leading and what He says in the Bible.

Really, Kristin's problem is a lot like many others we face constantly. Often there are things that are not clearly "wrong" or "right" but matters that must be investigated. We can easily be tempted to add extra rules to biblical womanhood—and I believe we ought to be careful there. But at the same time, if God is leading us to a certain conclusion, shouldn't we be willing to embrace it? No matter what our dilemma is—shouldn't His esteem be all that matters?

Whether you're wading through God's will, trying to figure out what's next for your life or how biblical femininity will play out in your day-to-day, Kristin's conclusion is a good point to end on. After weeks of deliberation, Kristin found out what she needed to learn all along: "I'm willing, more than willing, to live with disdain if it means I find my approval in Christ."

Ah. *That* is the right perspective.

Regarding
Dudes

"It will come about in that day," declares the LORD, "That you will call Me Ishi [Husband] And will no longer call Me Baali [Master]."
—HOSEA 2:16 NASB

If you could love me as a wife/and for my wedding gift, your life/should that be all I'd ever need?/ Or is there more I'm looking for?
—DEREK WEBB, "Wedding Dress"

CHAPTER 8

'Cause You
Need More
Than a Guy

Once upon a time, a girl named Rapunzel was held captive in a tall stone tower. Although she never escaped, through time she learned the key to contentment and lived happily ever after, alone. The end.

Yup, that's probably the stupidest paragraph I've ever written in my life. If my Rapunzel story were to aspire to true greatness, the heroine would have to have a rescuer, and he'd have to be cute. Every chick-lit author knows this. Every good country songwriter knows this. Without romance, the story has no appeal.

This mind-set is scarily contagious. I see it spill into my life all the time. We can start thinking that life is all about finding the "one," rather than loving the One who gave us the ability to love in the first place. Although loving "the Lord your God with all your heart, soul, and mind" is the foundation from which all other inner beauty grows, we can overlook its importance. I know I do.

As a little girl, I thought my life would begin the day my father walked me down the aisle. When I grew a little older, I realized that sounded lonely and pathetic, so I'd spout about how I might never marry and how Jesus' love was everything to me. But of course, that was a lie. Deep down, I suspected that my future husband would give me something Christ couldn't—something I needed. Even though this thinking is incredibly common among my friends, it's also incredibly destructive.

Take, for instance, a look at how it damaged the life of my friend "Leah."

IDENTIFYING RAPUNZEL

Leah was a dear girl, but she suffered from a disease that profoundly affected her teen years, inhibiting her single years. I call the disease "Rapunzel Disorder."

You might know of the disorder. Symptoms include overobsession with guys, insecurity about one's physical appearance, a desperate wish for male attention, and distraction from the wholehearted pursuit of Christ. Sound familiar? It may very well be. I haven't met a girl yet who is completely immune.

The consequences were dire for Leah. As a kid, she was the kind of girl everyone would've called independent and grounded, but when one boyfriend eventually expressed disinterest in her, Leah's "tough girl" mask began to crack. He didn't love her. After all this time of hoping and believing, Leah could hardly bear to consider that she had misunderstood his intentions.

Apparently the girl who proudly "didn't need" a husband was secretly captivated by thoughts of marriage, and a guy's love had become the purpose of her existence. No longer was Christ Leah's foremost love. She had surrendered His place in her heart and was left betrayed by the one who had taken His place. She was devastated. Her wounded condition was noticeable. At nineteen, she was ready to throw herself at the next guy who came her way—no matter who he was.

Earlier she had seemed so passionate for Christ. What had distracted her?

I found clues in remembering previous conversations with Leah and looking at the patterns of sin in my own life. It seems obvious that the disease grows when our gaze is shifted from Christ. It begins in the little things—the slight slanting of our thoughts toward "me, me, me," and not Him. Whether it's daydreaming about guys, feverishly planning a future career, or something as innocent as an obsession with reading romantic stories, we're sinning when *anything* else besides God becomes our main source of delight. It doesn't matter what it is. If any interest draws our eyes from Him, it's sin.

This isn't to pick on romance. Love is an amazing thing.

But Leah's desire for a glittery rock on her finger became too much when it kicked God from the "First Place" status in her heart. Marriage was no longer a girlish dream; it was an idol. Tim Keller defines an idol as "anything more important to you than God, anything that absorbs your heart and imagination more than God, anything you seek to give you what only God can give."[1]

No, I don't mean to pick on romance. I mean to pick on those dreams and pursuits that steal our eyes away from what really matters.

I have complete confidence that God can forgive Leah and help her to heal. I know our God can forgive all sin, but using God's forgiveness as an excuse to take sin lightly can have grave consequences. Leah is still facing repercussions from her obsession; years later, she's still trying to shed shame and regain lost feelings of worth.

What's the moral of this story? It's not to criticize Leah. Looking at her life, I realize how much she is like me. We both came from strong Christian families and have similar weaknesses. I could potentially walk in her shoes. I only share her story to reveal how *anything we choose to idolize on earth will eventually let us down.*

We will be left lacking and unsatisfied.

If you happen to have some experience obsessing over guys—or obsessing over anything self-oriented (be it beauty, popularity, reputation, or control)—I feel your pain. I've been there. Too often, I'm *still* there.

But as the clock ticks on, one must wonder if God has

something in mind for modern day Rapunzels besides twiddling their thumbs. There's got to be a better obsession for us to have. In the New Testament book of 1 Corinthians, the aim of unmarried women is explained:

> The woman who is unmarried, and the virgin, is concerned about the things of the Lord, that she may be holy both in body and spirit; but one who is married is concerned about the things of the world, how she may please her husband. This I say for your own benefit; not to put a restraint upon you, but to promote what is appropriate and to secure *undistracted devotion* to the Lord" (1 Corinthians 7:34–35 NASB, italics mine).

Notice those words "undistracted devotion." What does "undistracted" mean? What is "devotion"? And is that what you're currently giving to God?

A TELLTALE QUESTION

Do you feel like you will never be whole, never be complete without a husband? Do you yearn for the love and acceptance of others? Have you been searching for something that will give you a reason for existence and bring that spark of life to your eyes?

If you're there and you're obsessing over guys, you should know you've found a cause. But if you've been chasing it for long, you'll have noticed the trail of heartbreak it leaves behind. Guys will hurt you. Friends will leave. It's not that guys or friends are *out to hurt you*. It's just that because they're human, they're bound to disappoint. We all have our own set of issues, temptations, and weak areas. No matter how awesome a person seems in the beginning, the longer you travel down the road with him, the more his faults will be apparent. Never expect an imperfect person to be perfect; leave perfection to God. One special guy does not make a trustworthy cause. This cause doesn't satisfy either.

I could give you advice here, saying simply, "Let Jesus be your husband! Let Him fill that hole in you," except I'm not sure that'd be wise. The truth is, you *were* made for companionship. It was God who designed you that way. That's why God makes friends and community. It's one of the reasons God made marriage. Should you marry or live in singleness the rest of your life—you'll always feel that need to know and be known.

What I *have* learned and *can* say with confidence is, if all you have is Jesus—if He is your greatest love now and forever—you won't be settling for second best.

This is the truth I have to keep hammering into my own head: *Jesus is enough, Jesus is enough, Jesus is enough.* And He's not "enough" in that I'm-just-barely-getting-by, or He's-the-mud-puddle-I-play-in-while-longing-for-the-sandy-beach kind of way. He's enough in that He's *every-thing*. And when I love Him, He eclipses my every other need.

Pastor Matt Chandler once said,

> I have been a huge fan since my conversion . . . of men who wrote about God in such a way that is not friendship, and it's not cool and it's not something they like just . . . *like* . . . rather they have this burning, unsettling *lust* for the things of God.
>
> [It's just like David wrote in the Psalms:] "I yearn for You," "My flesh longs for You." . . . Or Brother Lawrence, in *Practice of the Presence*, who said, "I have had such delicious thoughts of the Lord that I'm ashamed to mention them."
>
> That's probably the most disturbing quote I have ever read in my life, and twelve years into my walk with Christ I still don't have a clue of what he was talking about. But it's there.[2]

God is *that* satisfying. Psalm 63:3, one of the most re-read verses in my Bible, says, "Because your steadfast love is better than life, my lips will praise you."

Loving God is your calling.
This is what your life was created for.

Ever been afraid of dying? Just think—God's love is *better* than life. If you had to die to find His love, death would be *worth* it. If you died only knowing His love, you'd have experienced an amazing life.

Are you lonely? Are you alone? Jesus invites you to be His friend—a friend He would die for. (He did.)

Are you grieving? No one heals like Jesus.

Are you a mess? No one tears out sin like Jesus. He fights for us—the real us that we're meant to be.

Most importantly, God created you for Himself. In the words of John Piper, "The reason God seeks our praise is not because He won't be fully God until He *gets* it, but that we won't be happy until we *give* it." God calls you to love Him, and He knows you won't be happy until you do. The fact that He wants your worship isn't arrogance on God's part. "This is grace," says Piper. "This is not egomania. This is love."[3]

See what I'm trying to say? Christ is enough. *Whatever* you're thirsting for, only Jesus gives real, soul-quenching satisfaction. Think of all He is. Don't be afraid to give yourself to that one Cause. He's worth it all.

Inner beauty does not exist without this principle. Purity, modesty, femininity—-all of this falls apart without this one heart condition: to be undistractedly, passionately, wholly, zealously, self-sacrificially, adoringly sold out *to enjoying and being enjoyed by our Savior.*

It's wonderful to memorize Scripture, to be a servant, and to tithe, to get married, and to [insert anything that sounds nice and/or holy], but those are all picture frames. They are meant to *accompany* the masterpiece and are useless without it. What does it matter to Jesus if you act like His worshipper, but inside it's actually dreams of a career/fame/fortune/husband that consume your thoughts?

Knowing Him is basking in
the fountain that spills over with
life, and knowing Him intimately
is diving more deeply
into who He created us to be.

The masterpiece—*the main thing that Jesus died to purchase*—is your soul. Loving God is your calling. This is what your life was created for.

PRACTICALLY SPEAKING:
LEARNING TO LOVE JESUS

Let's listen in for a moment on the last prayers of Jesus Christ before His crucifixion. He is about to pay the world's costliest ransom by suffering the world's most agonizing death. He is about to experience the taunts of both men and demons and—most horrible of all—the rejection of His Father.

With hands clasped, He prays.

Beads of sweat and blood rolling down His face, Jesus prays for *us*: "Father, the hour has come; glorify your Son that the Son may glorify you, since you have given him authority over all flesh, to give eternal life to all whom you have given him. *And this* is *eternal life, that they know You the only true God, and Jesus Christ whom you have sent*" (John 17:1–3, italics mine).

My soul, snap to attention. This is worth paying attention to. One does not simply *get* eternal life by knowing God. He *is* life. When Jesus reassured a tearful Martha that her dead brother would live again, He said, "I am the resurrection and the life; he who believes in Me will live even if he dies" (John 11:25 NASB). Notice that Jesus didn't say, "I'll *give* you life." He said, "You'll have life, and that life is Me."

Occupations, husband, children—all these are accessories to life. God is life itself. Knowing Him is basking in the fountain that spills over with life, and knowing Him intimately is diving more deeply into who He created us to be.

Joni Eareckson Tada wrote, "I want to know God like this! Shove me under the waterfall of the Trinity's joy, which splashes and spills over heaven's walls. If He's always in a good mood, I want to catch it. If I'm lost, I want Him to find me. Part the heavens, Lord, come down, kick aside the money tables, trash the 'Don't Touch' rules and embrace me."[4]

But how does one embrace *God*? How do we live

passionately for Him? A friend once told me about her struggles in this area. She said, "For a while, I'll be close to God, but then I start feeling alone. I become full of doubts and wonder if He's even there. Then He shows Himself to me and gives me peace, but then it starts happening again. It's an endless cycle of doubt." Her question was this: If I've already repented of my sin and committed to follow Him, how do I come to *know* Him? How do I become undistractedly devoted?

Loving Him is where it's at, so we've *gotta, gotta, gotta* learn how to get there. How do we get there—*practically?*

"TO DIE BY YOUR SIDE IS SUCH A HEAVENLY WAY TO DIE"

If you ever see a young couple in love, chances are it will be entertaining. It's funny witnessing two people totally distracted by each other. He hangs on her every word, while she wonders if she's ever laughed so hard at any other person's jokes or felt such deep sympathy for anyone else's problems. Their eyes meet constantly. The lovebirds are too preoccupied to notice if the restaurant closes or if the coffee has turned cold.

Not too long ago, my friends Josiah and Kessy fell in love. As a close friend of Josiah's sisters, I was over at the house all the time and witnessed the whole thing. Let me tell you, I've never seen so many adoring looks in one place before. If Kessy wasn't over at Josiah's, Josiah was constantly "at a concert with Kessy," or "at Kessy's church," or "over at Kessy's little brother's birthday party." When they weren't doing something together, they were calling each other. There is even a rumor that one party read aloud a novel to the other over the phone. Ah, young love. (Note, I'm saying this as a very single person who can't really understand that kind of infatuation yet. They tell me my time will come.)

Whether they realize it or not, the young-and-in-love couples of the world have learned valuable information on knowing the heart of God. When people are in love, they naturally desire to spend every waking moment together. Words that do not come easily in conversation with others are freely spoken. The same goes for God (James 4:8). If we want to know God more and thus love Him more, we must seek Him out. We must make time for Him, pray to Him, and savor His words like ice water in high summer.

This is such a basic truth, but one easily forgotten. A close, intimate relationship with God cannot be had unless it is based on spending time in the Bible. If we don't spend time with Him, we can't fall more deeply in love with Him.

The kind of Bible study I'm referring to isn't just one surface-level, thirty-second Bible reading per day. I'm talking about sincere Bible study, in which the Bible is read book by book, chapter by chapter, with time soaking in the truth in each verse.

There are different methods for Bible study, but the one I have found particularly helpful and reliable is expositional study. What I mean by "expositional" is basically the opposite of the Bible study method I used as a little kid, which then meant closing my Bible and reopening it to a random page that I'd skim through, pick out my favorite parts from, and then conclude my "study." There's trouble with that tactic because it can lead to reading verses out of context and not getting their full meaning.

Expository Bible reading, on the other hand, means reading a book of the Bible verse by verse, word by word. For instance, if I were reading in Hosea, I'd start at chapter 1. I wouldn't skip to chapter 11 (which is my favorite part of Hosea). Why? Because if I just skipped around and read random Bible verses, I couldn't understand what was really going on. I couldn't understand the magnitude of what God declares in chapter 11 because I didn't understand the opening scene of chapter 1.

This is just common sense. Who starts reading a book in the middle, anyway? It's an important thing to note, though, because if we only read bits and pieces of the Bible, we can easily misunderstand it. Expositional study means that we read and study all of the Bible, including the verses we wrestle with and find difficult to understand.

And that's what a lot of Bible studying is—wrestling. Whenever I sincerely read my Bible and think about how it applies to my life personally, I get uneasy. Often I'm convicted of an area in which I need change. Even though there's a lot in the Bible that can give us immediate joy, it also contains a lot for us to grapple with.

THEOLOGY: THE FAITH
ON WHICH WE STAND

Theology is a big part of that wrestling.

Okay, a warning here—I am now stepping on one my favorite soapboxes. And I'm not jumping on this topic because I love it but because I see it as so necessary. I say this with the same vehemence I'd use to tell a friend who's a smoker that she's going to ruin her lungs. Theology is of *the same* life-and-death-importance, if not much, much more.

I have friends who are afraid of the word "theology" because of the idea that theology or "doctrine" is something derived from human beings, that it's a list of legalistic concepts invented by a bunch of cocky scholars from the fifteenth century. In reality, theology isn't something invented by men. It's defined literally as "the study of God," and it's God Himself who gives us the primary source of our knowledge. Christian theology should start and end with studying the Bible.

Theological questions involve the person and nature of God. Usually we identify it with the "dry" stuff—like whether God is all-powerful, all-knowing, and really in control. But when you get into the "black holes" of life, and your mom breaks her back or your brother is helicoptered to the hospital, theology ceases to be dry. It becomes foundational, the cleft of the rock in which to hide your soul.

Once a girl told me that she didn't care about getting

deep in theology because she was happy to "just love Jesus"—as if loving Jesus and learning about Him could possibly be separated. How can someone really love someone else unless they take the time to get to know that person?

Imagine a guy saying to his girlfriend, "I love you more than life. You are so precious to me, but I also have my career, my daily routine, my love of sports, and my dog. I just don't have time for you. I hope you're okay with it if I just keep your photo in my wallet. I'll be sure to look at it whenever I forget what you look like. Although my schedule is jam-packed, honey, I think I can fit you in for a little while on Sunday mornings and Wednesday nights. Honey . . . honey! Where are you going?" The man would be insane to think the girl would still *be around* by Sunday.

No, if that guy loves that girl, he's going to hunt her down, research her favorite activities, quiz her friends on her favorite movies, and become an expert on her life story. 'Cause we all know, if you love someone, you get to know his or her details.

Yet by contenting ourselves with surface-level knowledge of God or waiting for a time in which we "experience" Him, we're essentially making the same mistake as that guy. We're trying to tuck God into a corner until it's convenient to pull Him out. When we refuse to care about theology, we're refusing to care about the nature of God.

CAN WE KNOW GOD?

Of course, there is a lingering question of whether God *can* be known. We're not just talking here about befriending someone we can see and touch. We're talking about befriending the invisible God of the universe. Isn't it a bit arrogant to assume we can actually *know* Him?

We can go way beyond surface knowledge; we can know God intimately.

A story is told about a group of blind men who discovered an elephant. Since the men were blind, they could only feel the elephant and guess what it was. As one man touched the elephant's tusk, and another touched its trunk, and yet another touched its leg, each came to different conclusions about what the animal was. Some people use the story of the blind men as a metaphor for human beings' attempts to know God. They say, "Well, since we're all basically stumbling around in the dark and each only know little portions of reality, we can't really understand the truth. We can't be confident that we *really* know God."

I like what Pastor Kevin DeYoung pointed out about this picture. He said that for Christians, something amazing has happened in our ability to understand truth. In our case, we're not groping in the dark to understand reality. The elephant has actually *spoken* to us. "Quit calling me crocodile or peacock or paradox. I'm an elephant, for crying out loud! That long thing is my trunk. That little frayed thing is my tail. That big floppy thing is my ear." Pastor DeYoung elaborated: "And what if the elephant gave us ears to hear his voice and a mind to understand his message (cf. 1 Corinthians 2:14–15)? Would our professed ignorance about the elephant and our unwillingness to make any confident assertions about his nature mean we were especially humble, or just deaf?"[5]

God Himself has written us a book to explain who He is, and He gave us in-depth detail. He didn't just write a one-page letter saying, "Hi, I'm God, and I love you." He told us stories. He gives a lot of heady information to help us understand our history, the world, and most of all Himself, so that we can know about this God who loves us. We can go way beyond surface knowledge; we can know Him intimately.

REWIND

You may be thinking, "So we've got to spend time with God reading the Bible each day—and that's it? *That's* the key to knowing the Creator of the universe?" It almost sounds too easy, if we forget that loving is giving and giving has never been a strong point of the human race. I resent giving up the last dinner roll, let alone my heart. Selfishness runs deep in our veins. We don't *want* to enjoy God (though He is the source of all *real* delight). We prefer to enjoy ourselves.

We don't jump up in the morning screaming like Buddy the Elf from the movie *Elf,* "I *love* Him!" At least, I don't. Steady, daily surrendering of ourselves is what is required to love Him more, and it isn't ever easy. Not even for martyrs.

LOVE IS WORK
(and Here Are Some People
Who've Dedicated Their Lives to It)

Occasionally there are human beings whose actions are so unselfish that the whole world gasps for a moment and stares. It's not because those people missed out on the selfishness gene, but because they've discovered the love that is more important.

I want to be like them.

Their names are immortal.

Jim Elliot: An American missionary, speared by Indians in Ecuador while attempting to share the gospel.

Lady Jane Grey: A seventeen-year-old English girl who bravely faced execution rather than forsaking Christ.

Stephen, the first martyr: A Jewish Christian stoned to death for his bold proclamation of Christ's teachings.

Watchman Nee: A Chinese man sold out to Christ,

who was imprisoned until his death.

All died, rather than forsake Christ; all possessed a passion for Jesus that permeated their entire lives.

When we hear their stories, do we ignore them? Do we say, "Wow, that's amazing, but I could never be like them"? Or are we inspired to investigate further and ask what caused these simple, normal people to be so zealous?

I suspect Jim Elliot, Lady Jane Grey, Stephen, and Watchman Nee had something in common. Instead of the flannel-board figure from Sunday school, with the bright blue eyes and perpetual smile, they saw Jesus as He really is. They spent time with the Son of God, and their lives were forever changed.

These heroes are mostly remembered by their last stand, the moment that etched their names in history. However, I suspect we miss out by reading about the ends of their lives before the beginnings. Each of these martyrs, at one point, struggled as every Christian struggles. They fought to be faithful to God.

Jim Elliot cried out to God in his diary to strengthen his passion for Christ: "'He makes His ministers a flame of fire.' Am I ignitable? God deliver me from the dread asbestos of 'other things.' Saturate me with the oil of the Spirit that I may be a flame. But flame is . . . often short-lived. Canst thou bear this, my soul, a short life?"[6]

Right after we are saved, loving Christ seems simple. But as time passes, we come to the painful understanding that our hearts wander. Our affections aren't steady. As we can tell in the quote from Jim Elliot, learning to love Him *deeply* requires continual surrender—continual work.

It sounds terrible, I know. Loving Christ is *work*? A struggle?

Absolutely.

It's a *trek* to wade through the heart, searching out sin in order to repent; it's no piece of cake to praise Christ while in tears, instead of indulging in the easy route of self-pity. Rotting in sin is definitely the easy way out.

Like the song says, "I have no fear of drowning; it's the breathing that's taking all this work."[7] It's not the initial leap off the diving board that's the most difficult part; it's losing what comes naturally and learning to breathe underwater. Now *that's* hard.

CONSISTENCY (and Discipline) IS EVIDENCE YOUR LOVE IS REAL

Remember that couple in love? You know, the duo who hung on each other's every word and whose example we should follow in pursuing Christ?

Suppose they marry and soon their initial love loses some of its novelty. He ticks her off by growing a mustache. She frustrates him by denting the car. He forgets her birthday. She burns the roast. No longer does her heart jump whenever he's near, nor does he always pay attention when she shares her opinion.

They've reached the point where keeping their relationship strong isn't simply a matter of going on another date. The two must both work at it. Although their marriage is no longer the idyllic "happily ever after," I think I could take a few pointers from their example.

I am emotional. Blame it on being a girl if you wish. It's not a bad thing, but it can be a hindrance if I allow my emotions to rule me.

It was a smooth ride for the first few days after becoming a Christian because I was in such a joyous mood. Paint my face yellow and call me a human smiley face, because I was happy, happy, happy. But the moment I felt depressed again was akin to stepping out of a car accident, looking at the twisted metal of my Christian life, and wondering how on earth I'd gotten into a wreck. What had I done wrong? Had God left me to fend for myself? My prayers became panicky. "God, where are You?" My steps of faith took place on wobbly knees. "God, can You even hear me?"

My faith had slipped into the wrong place. Instead of sitting securely on God's Word, my trust was in how I *felt*. I wasn't clinging to what one man called "the objective realities." Francis Schaeffer wrote, "With none of us is the way of going on steady. . . . But neither must we panic. . . . Remember . . . that even in the midst of the storm His promise is true: He holds us fast." [8]

It's natural to have icky moods, but we must *remember*. We must remember God's love and God's goodness even when we cannot feel them. We must *know* them.

We must *keep* reading our Bibles. We must *keep* praying

to God. We must *keep* remembering His goodness.

If my belief was where it ought to have been, I would have turned to the Bible first, before my emotions. Then I could've leaned on His comforting words: "If I should say, 'My foot has slipped,' Your lovingkindness, O Lord, will hold me up. When my anxious thoughts multiply within me, Your consolations delight my soul" (Psalm 94:18–19 NASB).

Like the married couple, our relationship with God will not grow if we base it entirely on our feelings or if we neglect the "discipline" aspects of knowing God—like prayer and studying His nature. Remaining close to Him requires dedication that can't be swayed, regardless of our moods.

Pastor C. J. Mahaney said it well:

> I'm not advocating that we completely ignore our feelings. Nor am I criticizing genuine spiritual experience. . . . it's just not where we're meant to begin. . . . When you read or hear Biblical truth proclaimed, what internal conversation takes place in your soul? Is your first reaction, *what do I feel about this?* If so, do you plan to continue submitting everything ultimately to your feelings? Or will you instead trust God's testimony, so that whenever you encounter Biblical truth your initial question will always be, *do I believe it?*[9]

It's struggles like these that keep the Christian life hard work, yet it's also *working* on relationships that makes them vibrant. After all, a friend is only an acquaintance until you've battled together for a cause. Once you've crawled through muddy trenches, faced bullets, blood, and an onslaught of enemy troops—that's when you become inseparable. That's why strangers can become like brothers in war.

Right NOW has Christ's name written all over it. Living passionately for God starts at this moment.

I can say with confidence that Jesus is more than a friend now that we've fought together daily for His place as first in my heart.

Unfortunately, there are some who see struggles ahead and shudder in fear. Toy soldiers are all they aspire to be, rather than the real deal. They become satisfied with fake Christian living. But these people are risking more by not pursuing Christ. They're not only risking their intimacy with Him, but they risk wasting their lives cowering in a bunker.

RAPUNZEL'S RESCUE

We last met Rapunzel in her tower, crossing out dates on her calendar as they rolled by. She still spends her spare time (which is actually *all* of her time) reading romance novels, watching chick flicks, singing tragic love songs, adding to her hope chest, and—oh yes—counting the days until Prince Charming's extremely manly face pops up at her window. (Pardon the cheesy imagery. You see what I'm saying.)

It makes me wonder, if Rapunzel lives only for some future day when the prince will make his debut, then where are the current hours, days, and weeks going? If those moments are spent on daydreams, she's sending her unmarried life down the tubes. She's wasting time with the hope that, upon Prince Charming's arrival, she'll suddenly know how to live, when the living is *now*.

Elisabeth Elliot wrote;

> Single life may be only a stage of a life's journey, but even a stage is a gift. . . . *This* gift for *this* day. The life of faith is lived one day at a time, and it has to be lived—not always looked forward to as though the "real" living were around the next corner. It is *today* for which we are responsible. God still owns tomorrow.[10]

It's tempting to live for marriage. Love is such a glorious thing! How can we *not* look forward to it? However, if God meant women to live only for marriage, we would have been born on our wedding day. Rapunzel would've been born the second Prince Charming spied her tower.

Instead, today isn't a "waiting period" before real life begins. Right *now* has Christ's name written all over it. Living passionately for God starts at *this* moment. Joy and satisfaction can be found in God *today.* I love what C. H. Spurgeon wrote, determining to make the most of his time: "The truest lengthening of life is to live while we live, wasting no time but using every hour for the highest ends. So be it this day."[11] And so be it tomorrow, the next day, and the next.

I've been saving myself for you, just you, no one but you/I've saved my heart in your name/ It's for you to claim/ Some day.

—ELLA FITZGERALD

CHAPTER 9

Purely
Yours

It led to one of the most humiliating moments of my childhood. As soon as I'd turned eleven, Mom decided to enroll me in speech and debate class. It was a good idea on my mom's part, but I still wish she had stuffed me in a closet for a few more years until my people skills developed.

It led to one of the most humiliating moments of my childhood. I clutched my backpack and hesitantly stepped into the classroom. I took a seat. The knots in my stomach began to unwind; I was going to be fine. In fact, this was my chance to be a star, my chance to shine. In fact . . .

The teacher's voice popped my reverie like a balloon. "Now, I will be assigning each of you with debate partners. You will spend time together preparing a case for the end-of-semester debate." All twenty pupils gasped in unison. Some of the girls giggled as the boys shifted in their seats.

One by one the teacher listed off partners, seating them at different tables until three names remained on her roster—two boys and me. "Hannah Farver, you'll be partnered with Eric Tyson." I could've sworn one of the flirtier girls in the room was about to faint. Hannah Farver partnered with Eric Tyson?! He was one of the "coolest" guys in our grade. This was going to be an interesting combination.

Right about that same time, I'd been forming an odd personal habit. Whenever my brother or sisters made a joke, I winked. Whenever I laughed, I winked. Whenever someone smiled at me, I winked. Can you see endless potential for embarrassment on my horizon? I only wish I had at the time.

We were having a good day in class. Thus far, I had survived debate. Life was going well. In all honesty, I don't exactly remember the circumstances of that fateful moment. Maybe one of the girls in the room had made a joke. Whatever happened was eclipsed in my memory by the next second. Smiling contentedly at whatever had transpired, I turned around toward Eric. He was laughing. I laughed too. Then, unconsciously, the eyelashes on only one of my eyes brushed my cheek. A wink.

I was dead.

I felt as though I had jumped off a diving board into a cement pool. Blood rushed to Eric's face at the same moment the blood rushed out of mine. My reputation and my life as I knew it were ruined. I felt like rushing out of the room to collapse in the safety of the girls' bathroom, but all I could do was look down.

For months after that, I would kick myself (literally) at the memory of the event that scarred my childhood. We were at the awkward, "I'm not sure what do around the opposite gender" stage anyway. Even now, I still wince and have to talk myself through it. ("It's okay, Hannah. You were eleven or twelve. No one remembers that day but you.")

Why do I bother telling that story? Because I am confident I am not the only person on the planet to have ruined her life at age eleven and certainly not the only girl who has struggled to find her way in the area of guy/girl relationships.

A COMMAND

Reading diary entries from my early teen years, I find one prayer is repeated over and over: "Lord, help me be pure." Entry after entry, I scribbled that prayer. Yet comparing that prayer to the fits of confusion, gossip, and crushes in my other entries, it's clear: I was clueless.

What exactly is purity? Tough to say, because there isn't a glossary in the Bible where we can look up that word. To muddy the waters more, there have been perfectly well-meaning writers and speakers in recent years who've complicated the definition by putting together romantic terms like, "saving your heart for your husband," or "not giving pieces of your heart away."

Really, I'd like to ask them what that means. The metaphors they use sound nice and make purity sound super romantic, but they don't mean a lot when we take them apart. Never did I read that phrase on a T-shirt and say, "Oh! Now I get it! Saving my heart. It's like . . . saving trees . . . and money . . . and baby seals . . . but with my heart. Everything is so clear now!" (To get its full glory, read that last sentence aloud with your best Brian Regan impersonation. If you don't know who he is, YouTube is your friend!)

Because when we're standing in the grocery store, arguing with our minds for one good reason not to fall head over heels with the bag boy, "saving your heart" just doesn't cut it.

As people created uniquely by God, we come complete with our own set of weaknesses and strengths.

Another common trend in the Christian community is to quote the Song of Solomon to give support and an explanation for purity—especially Song of Solomon 2:7 (NIV), which says, "Do not arouse or awaken love until it so desires." I'm not sure that verse is even *about* purity at all.

I *do* believe that there are verses in the Song of Solomon that strongly indicate that we ought to seek purity, but, really, you'd think that in an area so vital, God would've given us more information than a *single verse* in the Song of Solomon. And, you'd also think that if God took the time to put together thousands of pages for us to read, He would've given more detailed guidance in the area of our love lives. He says clearly we shouldn't have sex outside of marriage (Hebrews 13:4; 1 Corinthians 6:9–10), but other than that rule, purity can be mystifying. Why not provide some pointers?

At the same time, it can be a struggle to *find* verses on purity. If you look up the word "abstinence" in the Bible, you won't find it. If you look up purity, you'll find verses that have to do with seeking after holiness—not necessarily how we should handle ourselves around guys. But if we just look up those keywords, we may miss the fact that God has given us guidance—not only a few random verses—but *detailed* guidance for our behavior toward others.

LET'S ASK A DEAD DANE

Søren Kierkegaard, the Danish philosopher, once tried to figure out how a Christian was supposed to spend his or her life. In true philosophic style, he imagined a scenario to illustrate his question.

Søren pictured a man approaching him to ask, "What should I do with my life? Should I run for office?" In the scenario, Søren replied simply, "No, seek first the kingdom of God."

The man then asked, "Should I sell all my possessions and give them to the poor?"

Søren replied, "No, you should seek first the kingdom of God."

The man still didn't get the point and asked again, "Well, should I give up my home and travel the earth proclaiming the gospel?"

Søren said, "No, seek first the kingdom of God."

The same answer was given each time and fit each situation. The point wasn't that the man could never run for office or never become a missionary; those are good things to do. Søren was trying to make a broader point.

Whatever we're
doing in relation to romance
—is it seeking Christ first?

When deciding how to spend our lives, our first goal shouldn't just be to pick what sounds most spiritual or most pious. Rather, we should look to whatever opportunity would give God the most glory—what would advance His kingdom the most.

"Seek first the kingdom of God." Those weren't words originally coined by a Danish philosopher. They are the words of Christ, fit for application to the life of every one of His modern-day followers (Matthew 6:33).

I suspect the same concept translates to the purity issue, too. If we ask, "When I'm ready for marriage, should I date or court?" the answer should not come from what those around us consider the "normal" approach or what we consider the most "spiritual"-sounding tactic. The answer should come from the quietness, when we implore scripture and pick the brains of the wise Christians God has placed in our lives. The answer should come after we examine our lives and ask, "What would glorify God the most?"

Instead of, "Do I need a purity ring?" "Should I hold hands with him?" "Is it all right to kiss before marriage?" we need to ask the right questions: "What plan of action would God honor?" "Am I seeking the kingdom?" Therein lie our answers.

PRACTICALLY SPEAKING

So what does seeking first the kingdom look like practically?

Practically seeking God's kingdom can be widely varied for each person. The longer I live (which, I freely admit, hasn't been that long), the more I realize that obeying God can look different in different situations As people created uniquely by God, we come complete with our own set of weaknesses and strengths. When I try to seek first God's kingdom, I have to keep in mind my weaknesses in order to be wise, but since my weaknesses are not necessarily yours, our paths may look different. See?

Ultimately, we've all got to ask ourselves if *whatever* we're doing in relation to romance—is it seeking Christ first? Are we walking in wisdom? Are we pursuing God's best?

I'm not talking about launching into a dating versus courtship debate about or purity rings. I'm asking, "How are your motives? Are you wanting a relationship for a relationship's sake? Are you seeking love because you feel a need for male attention? Or is your first goal to follow where Christ leads?"

Just think for a moment, 'cause it all comes down to this: Are you doing what you're doing because your *first* priority is to glorify Him, or are you just following the pattern set by people around you? Are you seeking first the kingdom of God? And do you think you're truly *succeeding* in this—in bringing God glory—or are there things that you maybe need to change?

LET'S COOK UP A DEFINITION

As we go about asking what purity looks like, let's try to concoct a definition of purity. So far, we have decided that purity is seeking first the kingdom of God in our relationships.

Can we take this further? If God's first command for us is to seek Him first, then what's next?

Luke 10:27 puts it plainly: "Love the Lord your God with all your heart, soul, mind, and strength, and love your neighbor as yourself" (paraphrased). Really, it's another spin on the "seek first the kingdom" command, but it pulls love into the picture.

If you think about it, seeking first the kingdom of God *includes* loving your neighbor as yourself. And often the way we seek first the kingdom of God is *by* loving other people.

This verse has been a huge help for me in defining "purity." I'll show you what I mean:

Is premarital sex okay?

Well, is it loving your neighbor?

Is lusting after someone okay, because it only takes place in the mind?

Is it loving your neighbor?

Not only are lust and fornication mentioned in the Bible as being sin, they reflect a wimpy view of love. Premarital sex comes from a kind of "love" that says, "I'll be with you for this one night, even though we're not married and I have not officially vowed to stick by you for better or for worse *and* I may not even be interested in you in the morning. I just want to be gratified."

As Jesus said, "Everyone who looks at a woman with lustful intent has already committed adultery with her in his heart" (Matthew 5:28). The person who is technically "pure" in body but daydreams about enjoying romance with a person who isn't their spouse is in sin.

And what does lust communicate about our priorities?

Lust says, "I don't care that you're a creation of God or that you're a brother or sister in the Lord. I want to imagine committing sin." Not only is that disgusting, it's not love at all. Instead, it's using someone as entertainment. It's not seeking Christ first.

See how the "seek first the kingdom" and "love thy neighbor" verses can work as a test of our purity?

Romance is a good thing—
and God is the Giver of good stuff.

SPEAKING (Even More) PRACTICALLY

What about something less straightforward? What about flirting? What's so wrong with it?

Honestly, I have a hard time defining "flirting." I don't think good-natured banter is wrong. Humor is also a good thing. But I think we can all agree that flirting is different from just joking around.

The word "flirt" comes from the old French phrase *conter fleurette*, which means "to seduce by whispering sweet nothings."[1] It's the kind of "banter" and "joking around" that leaves a mark on you after the conversation has ended—so much you can't stop thinking about the person you were with at the time. You know your friendship isn't the same because in a way, somehow, you tried hard for his attention—harder than you would if you were "just friends."

Flirting is teasing that tries to attract the other person's attention as much as possible (and often, but not always, to draw attention to one's body). It's dropping little hints here and there that you just might be interested in that guy. It may be that like the adulteress in Proverbs 7:21, "with much seductive speech" you've drawn him in, and now you know he's yours. You've flattered and toyed with his emotions so much that you own him; he'd do whatever you ask.

And why is that bad?

It's not a big deal at all . . . *unless* you think that the people around you are real and valued by God. If that guy is a Christian, then he's your brother in the Lord. He's God's son. God died for him and is jealous for his worship. God wants to use that guy to do great things for His glory.

Are you playing with him or using his attention to make you feel better about yourself? Are you using his interest to bolster your pride? The answer may hinge on how you respond to those questions.

Does flirting advance the kingdom of God? You tell me.

TRUSTING GOD FOR GOOD THINGS

If we don't flirt, how will we ever find husbands? If we don't throw ourselves at guys, how will the right one ever notice us?

You may never wonder about this kind of thing, but I

certainly do. Here's what God continues to remind me:

Romance is a good thing—and God is the Giver of good stuff (James 1:17). If He truly loves His children, why then does God ever withhold romance from us? Why does He choose for some women to live as singles, while He chooses marriage for others?

There are a lot of "good things" I want. Ideally, I'd like my pick for the presidency to win the election. I'd like a full-ride scholarship to the college of my choice. I'd like to be given a yacht by some millionaire, cruise around, and then sell it for charity. I'd like for my future husband to arrive here . . . now! Those are all good—at least in my self-centered, shortsighted opinion.

I don't honestly expect a yacht or a full-ride scholarship. While I believe God *could* give me those things, I understand that God isn't my genie who offers me three wishes. In fact, demanding what I want from the God of the universe is just a little bit presumptuous, even arrogant, because in doing so I'm unconsciously saying that I'm a better life planner than He is. It's pushing my palm in God's face, saying, "I want what I want, and nothing You say can change me."

Yet if Jesus Christ loved me enough to die for me, and since He promises to nourish and cherish me, how can I fear His gifts? Why do I fear that what He'll give me is less than what is best? It's not difficult to understand why He's trustworthy, in light of how much He loves.

If God wants me to marry Mr. Fill-in-the-blank, then let

Him plan the details and the timing. If I can trust Him with my soul, I can trust Him to introduce me to the right guy.

Of course, that's not all. Once I start trying to trust God, my mind fills up with fear. I don't give up control that easily. I worry. What if what's best for me is unpleasant? What if He lets me peek at the gift He's sending me, and it includes suffering and loneliness—things I don't want? My hands are tied, since God doesn't provide gift receipts or offer refunds. What if, oh, horror of horrors, God wants me to be single? *Forever?!*

Honestly, it's not something I like thinking about. Life as a single woman would not be a fudge sundae for a person like me, nor I suspect for anyone else. There would be the struggle of loneliness, and it would require constantly falling on God for encouragement and comfort. Yet I'm confident that if a life of singleness is what God gives me, it is still the gift that is *best* for me, and that He would give me the grace to receive it. I choose to trust that whatever God gives will be the ideal, in the end. Because "good things" are not necessarily the *best* things, and God never withholds "good" from His children unless He sees something better on the horizon.

X + Y = -7
(You and I Aren't Algebra)

Another important reminder here is that God doesn't treat us like mathematical equations. He doesn't say, "Hmm

. . . Hannah needs to be less of a germaphobe. I'd better give her a husband that will plague her to death by never taking a shower. Okay, I'll make her marry sloppy George. Muahahaha." (Believe it or not, I've fantasized that scenario several times.)

God isn't unfeeling. I like what Suzanne Hadley wrote about this, when she pointed out that although we are God's tools to bring Him glory, we are *also* His beloved children:

It's true that God may set us apart for a season of singleness, but that doesn't mean He is indifferent to our dreams.

Matthew 7:11 (NIV) says, "If you, then, though you are evil, know how to give good gifts to your children, how much more will your Father in heaven give good gifts to those who ask Him!" God views you as a cherished child—never a utilitarian object. A loving Father will give you good gifts at just the right time.[2]

When we feel that God has short-changed or neglected us, we need to spend some time remembering that we're His beloved. And God doesn't ever lose track of those He loves. He knows our every heartstring as much as He knows how He created us. Whatever gifts He bestows are really, seriously for our good, even if we cannot see it at the moment they're given.

It is doubtful that if God has planted in your heart a real desire for marriage, He'll withhold that from you. It's possible that He may do so for a period, but Paul says in

1 Corinthians 7:9 it is better for singles to go get married than spend their lives "burning" for married life. Just the same, the principle of trusting God no matter His timing or His gifts is one that applies to all matters of purity.

God has given us a world in which romance means living with uncertainty. We don't know what's around the corner. We don't know how our stories will turn out. We only know that, as Psalm 9:10 says, "You, O Lord, have not forsaken those who seek you." We need only to trust in Him for our tomorrows.

"LITTLE IMPURITIES"

Song of Solomon 4:12 speaks of how a young woman, when pure, is like a "garden locked." (See? I can quote Song of Solomon too!) More than giving her body to her beloved on their wedding day, she must protect her purity by protecting her affections. This begins by guarding the heart. Okay, I'll admit that "guarding your heart" sounds a lot like "saving your heart," a phrase I've belittled. But the word "guarding" is used widely in the book of Proverbs and fits this image from Song of Solomon about protecting the locked garden.

It's not that it's unwise or wrong ever to think about marriage. It's not wrong to want to get married. The problem is when we turn our emotions for a guy into idolatry. You know, the "I can't breathe without you" kind of mentality. (If that's an actual line from an actual song, please don't sue me, 'cause I'm a poor college student and you wouldn't get any money out of me anyway!)

Although physical lust is a common problem, for women there is also an equally formidable temptation for "emotional impurity." Emotional impurity involves allowing our hearts to center on one guy. And with the potential to destroy thriving young women, emotion run wild is not an enemy to ignore.

I remember my friend "Haley" speaking in glowing terms about her man. She had practically grown up with Chase; their families did everything together. Everyone assumed Haley and Chase would marry one day—everyone including Haley.

As she grew older, what Haley loved most of all about her relationship with Chase was that she was "completely pure." She was going to trust that God had picked Chase as her future husband. Wedding bells rang in her ears . . . until the day she found out Chase had proposed to Larissa, one of Haley's friends.

To say that Haley was upset would be the understatement of the century. She reacted with, "I thought this was Your plan, God! I thought I'd get married and life would be perfect! What happened?"

Although Haley had technically remained pure in body, she'd given in to idolatry. She had obsessed over Chase, focusing her thoughts, affections, and emotions completely on him.

My heart breaks for Haley. Her experience was gut-wrenching enough, and the fact that she had turned Chase into her reason for breathing only made it all the more difficult.

Haley's not the only one. There are dozens of girls I know who have fought to find the line between loving someone heart-and-soul and *not* making him into a god. I can't say, "Well, they should've known better," because I've faced the same problem. (In fact, I even wrote a poem about it, once, which one of my friends now chants back to me when she's trying not to obsess over a guy. One way to totally lose the drama of a poem is to have your friends chant it to you.)

Suffice it to say, there've been plenty of times when I have pinned my emotions on someone who is not mine. With a little encouragement, I could easily be in Haley's situation, retracing my steps, trying to find exactly where I lost my focus. Stories like hers can serve to remind us that little choices matter, so keep a healthy outlook concerning marriage and That Guy.

They don't sound like much—the little daydreams kept locked inside seem harmless. But the heart is the key to our actions. Little choices pack a punch. "Keep your heart with all vigilance, for from it flow the springs of life" (Proverbs 4:23). Even a "little" idolatry in the heart can grow into Godzilla.

Has your heart ever given an extra thump-thump when a certain guy's name is mentioned? (Note that this part isn't bad *at all*, but watch what can follow if we don't tread carefully.) Have you ever noticed that, even if he gives no sign whatsoever that there is any possibility for the two of you to be "something," you start thinking about him *all the time?* And have you noticed when that activity begins to take up *every neuron in your brain?* You start begging God for this guy's affection, planning your life around him, and neglecting the people and tasks God has placed around you *right now* because this guy has got your attention.

Don't feel like you're the only one. Don't feel like it's wrong to fall in love, either. What we have to be careful of is the tendency to throw ourselves into man-worship. We think that if we can only obtain *that guy*, our lives will be perfect. We'll be satisfied. At last, we think, we'll be able to enjoy life to the fullest.

From one hopeless romantic to another—let me warn you, *amiga*, that's a slippery slope! Idolize a guy now, and you'll become blind to his faults. You won't be able to see him as he is and love him as a real person. Instead, you'll love him as some made-up superhero your brain has created.

Not only that, but your relationship with Jesus will suffer. You'll find it harder to worship God on Sundays when the rest of the week your life revolves around that guy.

Point? We need to watch our little choices and be vigilant when making them. We're in danger if we let our emotions take the lead, without making sure we're walking hand in hand with wisdom. Never doubt that the "small" steps toward idolatry can have disastrous results.

No, romantic thoughts aren't wrong. It's just balance we need.

WHAT ABOUT THOSE SHADES OF GRAY?

We know idolatry is wrong—but where does it begin? When trying to understand purity, I desperately wanted someone to draw me a graph. "Show me EXACTLY where sin starts." I still haven't met a talented enough graph-artist to draw one for me (though I'm still accepting applications).

So what are we to do? How wise is it to nurture feelings for someone if they show no sign of feeling the same way? Are emotions altogether bad? I think my friend Lindsey summarized it well:

Feelings are wrong. Don't have them. Platonic friendships really rock. Determine to keep it that way forever. Guard your heart, girls, and don't ever let yourself think of a friend as a possibility. Right? *Buzz!* Wrong . . .

[Feelings are not inherently sinful.] In fact, to be blunt, we're not going to get married without them. The trouble only begins when we let ourselves experience the flutters of romance while we're too young for marriage—or, if we're eligible, when the object of our affections has not made a direct, clear initiation. Until then, our responsibility is to block out intrusive, categorizing thoughts. Every Christian young man that you encounter, regardless of how closely he aligns with your expectations for a future husband, is a brother. Period"[3]

Lindsey's offering smart advice, and later I'll talk about why I came to the conclusion that "direct, clear initiation" is important, but I think there's obviously a lot of room for confusion here. There's a lot of gray. When is attraction a part of God's exquisite love story that He's handwritten for you, and when is it an idolatrous detraction from the attention only God deserves?

There's no clear line I can define. All I know is that there is a line, and it is one best defined by the gentle prodding of the Holy Spirit. Take Elisabeth's story for an example.

PRACTICALLY SPEAKING: HOW ELISABETH LISTENED TO THE HOLY SPIRIT

Elisabeth was in love. There was no other way to put it. The college student hadn't expected to attract the attention of her athletic, plain-speaking classmate, but she had. And Jim was everything Elisabeth wanted. He noticed her quiet ways, and the fact that he memorized Bible verses in the cafeteria during lunch hadn't escaped her notice either. Jim was bold and strong, and Elisabeth found him difficult to forget.

On one trip out into the country with a group of friends, Jim stepped aside with Elisabeth and confessed that he was in love, crazy in love with her. But he was not free. Convinced of God's calling on his life to spread the message of Christ overseas as a single missionary, Jim doubted a wife was in his near future. He couldn't marry. Not yet—and maybe not ever.

While Jim may or may not have been wise in confessing his feelings to her when he wasn't yet available, it did throw everything out into the open. Jim and Elisabeth clearly had a problem. They were in love—but both felt instinctively that the timing was off.

It's not wrong to want to get married. The problem is when we turn our emotions for a guy into idolatry.

Elisabeth was torn. Her affections were Jim's, but a Greater Affection had long before arrested her soul. There was no law against Jim's love for her—no Bible verse forbade their attraction—but they each knew inwardly that now was not the time. Their budding relationship was, at the moment, only a source of distraction and heartache.

Elisabeth wrote later,

I wanted to be loved. Nothing unusual about that . . . But I [also] wanted something deeper. Down among all

the foolishness in my diary, thoughts like chaff that
the wind of the Spirit can drive away, there was some
wheat. There was an honest-to-God longing for the
"fixed heart."

Did I want what I wanted, or did I want what He
wanted, no matter what it might cost? Until the will
and the affections are brought under the authority of
Christ, we have not begun to understand, let alone to
accept, His lordship. The Cross, as it enters the love life,
will reveal the heart's truth. My heart, I knew, would
be forever a lonely hunter unless settled "where true
joys are to be found."[4]

There were no explicit Bible rules holding Elisabeth
back, except perhaps the one to "Love the Lord your God
will all your heart and soul and mind." She wanted to obey
that one verse above her feelings, even at the sacrifice of
loving Jim. Hers wasn't a legalistic restraint, only a personal
conviction to wait.

Pastor John Piper gets at the same problem of fitting
desire and unfitting desires:

Avoid as much as is possible and reasonable the sights
and situations that arouse unfitting desire. I say "possible and reasonable" because some exposure to temptation is inevitable. And I say "unfitting desire" because
not all desires . . . are bad. We know when they are
unfitting and unhelpful and on their way to becoming

enslaving. We know our weaknesses and what triggers them. "Avoiding" is a biblical strategy.[5]

So what do we know? We *know* that idolatry is wrong. When your affections become idolatry, or when you know in your spirit that your "crush" is premature and is on the verge of becoming guy-worship, you know troubled waters are ahead, if not already swishing around your ankles.

For a time, Elisabeth and Jim told themselves no. Though this "no" was sometimes intermixed with their hearts crying out for the opposite, and although she sometimes stuck to her guns with very little enthusiasm, Elisabeth slowly found herself dying to the idea of Jim. It's not that she loved him any less, but she could not demand her desires from God. She knew Him too well for that. She wrote in her journal, "My soul asks 'Why?' but then the quiet word, 'Wait thou only upon God.' And so not even for the light to show a step ahead, but for Thee, dear Lord, I wait."[6]

Sometime later, God gave the green light and Elisabeth happily became Mrs. Jim Elliot. But the moral of this story, for now, is not that they married. It's that they devoted themselves to God, even if that meant waiting on their dreams, simply because they heard the call of His Spirit.

This kind of desire for purity that does not depend upon rules, but rather on God's leading, is a call to us for maturity. To live it, we must be willing to submit to God. To understand it, we must be mature enough to avoid legalism (condemning other Jesus-followers who are in different situations) and have the patience to wait for the sound of His voice.

MARRIAGE:
ONLY THE MATURE NEED APPLY

Writer Josh McDowell said, "What you are as a single person, you will be as a married person, only to a greater degree. Any negative character trait will be intensified in a marriage relationship, because you will feel free to let your guard down—that person has committed himself to you and you no longer have to worry about scaring him off."[7]

It's all too easy to romanticize marriage, associating it with long, flowing wedding gowns, flowers, and diamond rings. A dear friend of mine isn't sure if she's ever meant to marry, but she's bought her wedding dress anyway. (I can't blame her—who doesn't like the idea of throwing a large party where you're bound to be loved and the center of attention?)

As much fun as a wedding ceremony will be one day, I don't want to allow myself to confuse a wedding with a marriage. After all, when the excitement of the wedding dies down, there will be laundry to do.

It doesn't require past experience to have a mature perspective on marriage. Just think about what marriage entails: responsibility, budgeting, cleaning, cooking, and in-laws— all of which may require a mature perspective to endure.

I love the idea of marriage. As the One who imagined marriage in the first place, God loves it too. Believing that marriage is a bed of roses, on the other hand, will only make the weeks after your wedding an unpleasant shock. Men and women are sinners who, well, sin. No marriage can completely measure up to marriage as God intends created. Having an unrealistic view of marriage doesn't help with purity either.

If your heart is flip-flopping a million miles per hour when you think of a certain guy, consider if you're actually ready to grow old with him. If you're not mature enough, or if the guy you're interested in isn't mature enough or in possession of a consistent, godly character, don't be fooled. It isn't time to "wake up" romance.

Marriage was created to echo God's love for the Church. In between the lines of Christian marriages, the world should be able to read a greater love story: the Eternal Romance between Christ and His bride (us). He pursued us, wooed us, sealed His commitment to us with His own blood, protects and leads us still. To reflect that love story *fully* is impossible, but to offer at least a dim reflection requires a firm commitment to purity.

Constantly falling for different guys by letting our hearts aimlessly wander before (or after) marriage does not echo the Eternal Romance. Consider: Is the church encouraged to love Christ and seek out other gods too? Are we allowed to kiss idols while claiming His Cross?

That's not the way love works at all. God desires us to

worship Him, and Him alone. Adultery is off limits. Christ alone died for our hearts; Christ alone *deserves* our hearts.

In the same way, a wife's heart belongs to her husband. There's no dating around when the marriage commitment is made. It's a commitment, a promise meant to be kept. Maintaining this realistic view of marriage is necessary for a purity-nurturing outlook.

WE WHO ARE BROKEN
SING SONGS OF GRACE

Talking about purity, it always brings to mind mistakes. Mistakes I've made. Thoughts I've had. Emotions I've wasted.

In reality, we all have reason to feel regret. Whether you feel guilty for a specific period of your life, for a specific action, or whether you've just wasted too much time idolizing the "one"—we've all fallen short of God's holiness. And I want you to be certain that no matter what you've done, no matter in what ways you've compromised your purity, that God can and does forgive. *You* are *not* unforgivable.

Not long ago, I heard my pastor, Matt Chandler, tell this story.[8] He'd met a woman who was a single mom and currently in an affair with a married man. Matt and his friends knew that she wasn't a follower of Christ, so they tried different methods of reaching out to her. One day they invited her to a Christian concert where they knew a preacher would be presenting a message. (It was all part of their master plan to go to a concert and then "sneak in" a sermon. Good, right?)

So Matt and his friends wound up in the audience, seated next to this girl who was living in sin and sincerely needing the love of Christ, when the preacher came onstage and started talking about . . . sex. In his hand, he held a rose symbolizing sexual purity. As his cool visual aid, the preacher passed the rose around the audience and had everyone touch it. Finally, in the course of his message, after explaining why it was so important to be pure, the preacher said, "Where's my rose? Someone give me my rose."

Someone in the audience gave him back the rose. The preacher held it high so everyone could see that, after being passed around so much, the rose was crumpling and falling apart. Its petals were drooping. It was worn-out.

And the speaker's crescendo—his main point—was "Look at this rose! Who would want this? Who would want this? It's like you when you sin sexually, when you pass yourself around."

Matt explained that at that point, seated next to this woman who had given herself away physically—his blood began to boil. He said that he wanted to scream out, "Jesus wants the rose!"

Jesus wants the rose!

We're *each* crumpled and dirtied by sin. Whether the sin has been impurity or other mistakes—we're each that rose. None of us is lovable. But that's the point! We're crumpled and unworthy. But Jesus wants the rose. Jesus wants us. Because He has this . . . *extravagant* love. He makes broken things new again.

Maybe you're a child of God, but you have a hard time believing that He loves you, that He could actually forgive you. Maybe you feel like the kid God invited in off the streets—like, He's nice to you but He couldn't possibly love or accept you as His *real* child.

Let me tell you, *if you have already confessed those sins and are committed to living a new life in Jesus*—that nagging feeling of condemnation is a lie. No matter if it's a preacher or a book or your own mind that taunts you with guilt—that guilt is a lie from the pit of hell. There is no condemnation for those who are in Jesus Christ (Romans 8:1, or, hey, just read the whole chapter).

You do have hope.

Is your soul battered by sin? Is your past like a bruise that won't go away? Good. Because Jesus saves and loves and *died* for people like you. He didn't come to save those who were too proud to recognize they needed saving. He came for the sick. He came for sinners like us. That's what the Gospel is all about. Jesus wants even us.

A Heart
Claimed by a
Radical Love

A bosom friend . . . you know—a really kindred spirit to whom I can confide my inmost soul. I've dreamed of meeting her all my life.

—ANNE IN L. M. MONTGOMERY'S *Anne of Green Gables*

Grace abounds/even for those who know better/than to bury such treasure/and I stand here as a witness to the sweetest affection—/the love of my brothers and sisters.

—THE NEW ATTITUDE BAND, "Grace Abounds"

CHAPTER 10

Another Love You Need

I was in the middle of a disagreement. Not an all-out war (though there were some injuries), but an awkward, too-polite-to-be-a-fight time with a friend. And it was festering. Planted on the linoleum of my bathroom floor, I gripped my toothbrush and used all that pent-up anger to scrub my teeth. (My poor enamel!) At the same time, my mind raced through all the words, spoken and unspoken, that had caused this volcanic eruption.

Suddenly, I stopped and spoke to the mirror. "Hannah, you'll have to face it. People will always break your heart."

I admit I was a little mad at the world. I wished I could just crawl in a cave and give up on friendships altogether. At that moment, friendships were so frustratingly painful they almost didn't seem worthwhile anymore. But I realized that if I pulled deeper into myself and truly did hide from my friends, I would become worse off. No matter how "annoying" people's differences can be, we need each other.

Worthwhile friends
help us keep the Cause
central in our lives.

Of course, it isn't just friends we need. We need the *right* friends. Aesop, the famous Greek storyteller, told a pithy story about the importance of good friendships, which goes something like this: "One day, a man was walking along a road when he saw a piece of clay in his path. He stooped to pick it up, and he smelled a sweet fragrance. 'This is but a piece of clay,' said the man in bewilderment. 'How is it that this scent is so sweet and fresh?' The piece of clay replied, 'I have dwelt with the rose.'"[1]

As the saying goes, "You are what you eat." Scarfing down jelly doughnuts does not make for a healthy heart; poring over trashy novels does not make for a healthy mind; spending hours in the company of a complainer doesn't make for a good attitude. The things we allow to influence us matter.

While it is important to reach out to those who are

unsaved or struggling in their faith, the truth is inescapable: the people with whom we spend the majority of our time will eventually influence who we are as individuals. Friends affect us, for better or for worse. First Corinthians 15:33 warns us: "Do not be deceived: 'Bad company ruins good morals,' " and Proverbs declares that those who spend their time in the company of the wise will become like the wise, and those who keep company with the foolish become fools (Proverbs 13:20).

It's important to surround ourselves with those who will spur us on to a mature, vibrant love for Christ. Worthwhile friends will help us keep the Cause central in our lives.

On the flip side, finding other God-seeking companions can be a struggle. For years (from when I was about eleven until I was eighteen), I'd periodically enter my mom's bedroom with a tearful confession of how lonely I felt without friends my age.

Sure, I knew some other girls. There was "Courtney," who liked to criticize the bodies of everyone else around her and once grabbed my wrist to tell me it was fat. There was "Alisha," who focused her time on chick-lit novels and was in love with Orlando Bloom. What was I supposed to do? These girls didn't seem to share my interests and passions *at all*.

Little did I know how many other young women felt just as isolated. I've spoken with countless girls since then who have voiced their frustration: "I can't find friends who are serious about their faith *anywhere!*" Maybe you can relate.

Each of us carries an innate desire for friendship—friendships that don't just result in the shallow, hollow chit-chat we often resort to, but that bloom with real, transparent discussions. Sometimes that desire for friendship is buried by loneliness. Sometimes we get used to being hermits and say we're "happy to be alone," though we weren't created to enjoy solitude for long. In fact, if we were honest, we'd realize we need someone who is willing to *pray* with us.

"Ordinary radical" Shane Claiborne has it right on that point:

> Community is what we are created for. We are made in the image of a God who is community, a plurality of oneness. When the first human was made, things were not good until there were two, helping one another. The biblical story is the story of community, from beginning to end. Jesus lived and modeled community with his little band of disciples. He always sent them out in pairs, and the early church is the story of a people who were together and were of one heart and mind, sharing all in common. . . .
>
> Everything in this world tries to pull us away from community, pushes us to choose ourselves over others, to choose independence over inter-dependence, to choose great things over small things, to choose going fast alone over going far together.[2]

Our spiritual selves need companionship. We need others to share our struggles and lift our eyes to hope, when we lack the courage to lift them ourselves.

But before we begin an interrogation of every female living in a thirty-mile radius and post want ads in the paper, we should first ask ourselves some questions. What makes a quality friendship? And where do we sign up?

MEET JULIE

Julie is your stereotypical teenage girl. If you see her, she will probably be texting one of her many "friends" on her cell phone. She's a social butterfly to the max, constantly out and about, storming a local shopping mall or catching a movie. Friendship, to Julie, is a relationship meant to supply fun to her life.

Julie has younger siblings she occasionally babysits, and her mom is often around the house, available for a conversation. While Julie thinks her siblings are cute most of the time and her mom isn't bad, she would die before considering them her friends.

Does Julie sound familiar? She does to me! When I was about fifteen or sixteen, she was the kind of girl everyone seemed to want to be: popular, nice, but not overly connected to her family. Perhaps she resembles some of your acquaintances. Perhaps she even resembles you.

Although I don't text my friends all the time (define "all the time"), I can identify somewhat with Julie. Her perspective on friendship is one I've definitely shared before. But there's a danger in her perspective: the focus is on "me." This approach to friendship says, "Friends are about fulfilling *my* needs for entertainment."

There is nothing wrong with shopping or going to the movies. I like doing those things every once in a while. The problem is that in our culture, we often think of friends as people we spend time with exclusively for amusement—and nothing deeper.

A friend once mentioned wistfully, "Wouldn't it be nice if our friends were not only people we hung out with but people we served God with?" It would not only be nice, it would be beautiful! Friendships are not designed solely to add fun to our lives but to draw us to God. In Hebrews 3:13, Christians are told to encourage each other: "But exhort one another every day, as long as it is called 'today,' that none of you may be hardened by the deceitfulness of sin."

Wait a second. If friends are supposed to exhort each other, that means they should speak on *spiritual* things, too. That means for a *true* friend, it's perfectly natural to ask how a Bible study is going. It means it's appropriate to *pray* together, share burdens, and express convictions. It's even appropriate to keep each other *accountable*, baring our souls about particular spiritual struggles and asking a friend for advice and to keep an eye out, making sure that we don't fall into sin.

In the past, some of the most precious time spent with friends at sleepovers did not include exchanging shocking secrets or gossip but instead conversation centered on our spiritual lives. I would, for instance, explain my feelings of frustration in learning to trust God with my worries. Amazingly enough, my friend would have coincidentally read about trust that very morning. Verses were shared; hope was refreshed. And something inside each of us cried out, "This is the way friendship is meant to be!"

LOVE ISN'T BLIND

We all recognize these words of wisdom from elementary school: "What's the vitamin for finding friends? B1!" It's common knowledge that to make friends requires *being* a friend, and to be a quality friend requires love. What is less known, however, is the difference between love and tolerance. The two are often confused for one another, when each is drastically different.

For instance, my parents used to often point out that I can be too quiet and private around the house. I prefer working alone, writing and reading books, and can sometimes be reserved. Although I did not mean to be rude, I *was* being selfish in keeping so much to myself. I was unconsciously pushing my family away, and they wished to be included in my life. It was completely reasonable for my parents to correct me in this area, and it was actually an act of love that they showed the problem to me, so that it could be fixed. But I couldn't see the extent of the problem for a long time.

I have a great friend who shares my name, so we call her "Hannah-chan" to keep ourselves straight. It was not until Hannah-chan spoke to me some months after my parents had mentioned my isolation tendency that the truth began to hit home. On a trip to the beach, she gently told me how she had seen a severe fault in me—the fault of being too private. She said she understood I was not trying to be unfriendly, but others would not always realize that, and it could damage my relationships with them.

At first, the truth hurt. Part of me wanted to deny what Hannah-chan said. I *couldn't* actually be antisocial! *Surely*, everyone could see my feelings as clearly on my face as I felt them. But, as days passed, I realized she was right. To expect my friends to read my thoughts was expecting too much, and I was selfish in allowing my moods to dictate how much conversation I shared with others. It was a serious character flaw, because it could give off the impression of arrogance (not that I'm without arrogance, but that's another story) or at least disinterest in the people around me.

Friends don't
let friends live in sin.

To understand what this confrontation meant, you must know Hannah-chan. She's one of the sweetest people

I know. (Think something sorta similar to Jane Bennet from *Pride and Prejudice*.) In conversation, she's always the first to encourage or offer a good opinion of someone. She's been known still to give someone credit for being "nice" long after I've become completely ticked at them. It must've taken a lot for Hannah-chan, because she is so merciful, to reveal her concern to me.

But Hannah-chan didn't leave the conversation there. Nearly a year later, she brought up the subject of my personality flaw again. This time, it wasn't a confrontation. Rather, she wanted to let me know that she had seen an improvement in my behavior. "Hannah, I just want to let you know that I've seen huge changes in you." She said, "You're not the same as you were before."

Although I haven't totally conquered this sin issue, her comment brought hope to my heart. What's more, Hannah-chan left a lasting reminder of what friendship should always be like.

NO TOLERANCE FOR TOLERANCE

The love Hannah-chan demonstrated is worth noticing and stands in contrast to mere *tolerance*. Where Hannah-chan spoke honestly from her heart, she could've simply swept the problem under the carpet. She didn't *have* to speak up. *Tolerance* can hide truth rather than risk any kind of conflict. For instance, when a friend stops reading her Bible and shows no sign of hunger for God, your desire to show tolerance may tell you, "Keep quiet. If you want to stay friends, don't speak up."

In the words of pastor and professor Voddie Baucham, "Tolerance has morphed into a big hairy monster that demands we not only put up with but even embrace and celebrate the views and practices of others. . . . This is the type of thinking that prompted G. K. Chesterton to exclaim, 'Tolerance is the virtue of a man without conviction.'"[3]

Those without conviction, or firm beliefs, are easily swayed to keep silent on important issues. But for quality friends committed to the well-being of their companions, this sort of tolerance shouldn't even be an option.

Of course I'm not suggesting that friends ought to nit-pick at each other's faults. But when a friend is clearly living in a way that opposes Scripture or when you see a negative trend developing in their lives (e.g., they have a growing distaste for spiritual things, or they're making excuses for sinful behavior), it is the responsibility of a true friend lovingly, privately to bring the matter to light.

Friends don't let friends live in sin. "Faithful are the wounds of a friend; profuse are the kisses of an enemy" (Proverbs 27:6). Real love can't simply ignore sinful behavior or tighten its lips when it sees something wrong.

At the same time, confronting a friend can be one of the most difficult things to do. Your friend may feel defensive or argumentative, and she may not initially receive what you have to say. The confrontation could mean that she will be icy toward you for some time to come. She might even drop the friendship altogether. Plus, as the confront*er*, you're going out on a limb, risking your friendship. You're speaking out, knowing full well that, in return, she may call *you* on the carpet for some wrong behavior. Confrontation isn't pleasant by any stretch of the imagination.

Quality friends offer rebuke.
And smart friends listen.

Clearly, such confrontation is something to be approached with caution, prayer, and the support of Scripture. We should avoid approaching friends with a rebuke unless we're certain the Bible backs us up. In fact, it's smart to bring specific Bible verses to our friends that address the issue they're currently facing. Laying it all out on the table allows a friend to see that we're not attacking her out of our own love for conflict—but that we see something is wrong, something that doesn't line up with God's Word.

I know from my own experience that living with a pattern of sin devastates my walk with Christ. If your friend is living with a consistent, overlooked sin, it *will* get in the way of her walk with Christ. When she attempts to pray, it will pull her mind away. The sin will steal her time and snag her feet along the journey. As someone who loves her, you *must* confront her on the issue because her spiritual health is at stake. By bringing the matter to her attention, you are saying, "I care more about your relationship with Christ than keeping my friendship with you. I am risking the loss of our friendship. I am speaking up because I don't want sin to drag you away from Christ. This issue concerns me, and it's only because I love you so much that I bring it up."

Quality friends offer rebuke. And smart friends listen.

This is also key: to be a good friend, you must not only give rebuke to others but be willing to accept it yourself. A friend probably won't offer gentle criticism if she thinks you'll retaliate by spamming her email address or slashing her tires. So make it clear you're open to receive correction where correction is due, and that your love for your friend will not change if she confesses some unpleasant truth.

In Psalm 141:5, King David prayed, "Let a righteous man strike me—it is a kindness; let him rebuke me—it is oil for my head; *let my head not refuse it.*" I suspect from these words that King David didn't seek his friends solely for their entertainment value. He didn't pick the funniest guy in the room to be his advisor. He longed for the kind of friends who would love him enough to wound his pride. He wanted friendships with righteous men, welcoming and *asking* for their rebuke, knowing that the end result would be the best for his soul.

BUT ISN'T THAT JUDGING?

What about the "j" word? You know . . . *judging?* How can you confront a friend without judging her? Truth be told, you can't. Don't shut this book yet. It's true—judging is a part of a healthy, Christ-honoring friendship. I love what my friend Lindsey once wrote on this issue:

It's possible that Christ's famous words from the Sermon on the Mount, "Judge not, lest ye be judged," may be one of the most over-used and misapplied verses in the Bible. Christ wasn't instructing us to halt discernment. If you look at the context of Matthew 7:1, Christ was speaking against the moral snobbery that peers down at fellow sinners, while imagining itself to be in the place of God— holy and blameless. In context, the verse instructs about checking ourselves for the same sin before we confront anyone else on it. It doesn't say we should avoid confrontation altogether.

Nowhere in the Bible is it remotely implied that it's our business to scorn weaker Christians and react without patience or compassion. Passing hypocritical judgment is a grave sin. . . .

At the same time, the whole of Scripture is abundantly clear that clear discernment between good and evil, truth and error, is an absolute necessity. Just a few verses after the "judge not" edict in Matthew 7, Christ talks about proper judging—by a person's actions, or "fruits." The Lord scolded the Pharisees, "Stop judging by mere appearances, and make a right *judgment*" (John 7:23–24).

Romans 12:9 exhorts, "Hate what is evil; cling to what is good," and if you read any of the apostle Paul's epistles, two things will leap off the pages: [Paul's] immense love for the churches he wrote to, coupled with unswerving commitment to preservation of the truth. That entailed kicking false teachers out of the Church and reproving the Christians when they strayed (just check out 1 and 2 Corinthians). In a word? . . . *judging.*[4]

Lindsey is right. I mean, just picture for a moment how different the church would be if we were able to freely confront each other about spiritual things, without putting up the automatic "you're judging me" wall. If, when others lovingly rebuked us, we didn't immediately accuse them of wrongdoing and instead investigated our own hearts, don't you think good things would happen? We'd grow. We'd love each other more selflessly. We'd approach sin with more trepidation. We'd be safer, because our Christian buddies wouldn't let us fall into sin without doing everything they could to pull us out.

FRIENDS IN UNEXPECTED PLACES

We can all imagine the scenario: You're sitting at a kitchen table, decked out in full tea-party attire (you know, the long, flowy skirt and big, gauzy hat). Old women sip daintily from china teacups around you at the table. Although much chatter is swirling about the room, for some reason you can't escape the uncomfortable feeling that much of the chatter is about *you.*

One woman shoots you an overly sweet smile as she passes a plate of cucumber sandwiches. "I remember changing your diaper when you were a baby." She cackles. "My, that was unpleasant!" The rest of the women twitter like hens over the joke. You shift in your seat, wondering what could possibly be next.

The woman nearest you pinches your cheek between her fingers. "Look how much you've grown! Why, I'll bet you have to beat the boys away from you with a stick!" Another lady adds, "Just remember something, honey. My son, Joel, he's real handy around the house . . . and single, too."

"Um, thank you." You smile politely, trying to remember if Joel was that boy who once chased you when you were a little girl, threatening to put crickets in your hair.

"In any case, you'll have to remember to name one of your children after me. You'll probably have several to choose from!" With that, your vision fades into a kaleidoscope of women laughing, giggling, and swallowing cucumber sandwiches in such frenzy that you almost feel like crying.

It's silly. I've never experienced such an awkward teatime scenario before; but the stereotype of "older women" still automatically triggers thoughts of a bunch of cantankerous matchmakers whose greatest joy is found in gossip. There's that idea, or it's easy to picture a group of women looking down their noses, eager to condemn anything we do. They're quick to say, "Thou shalt not," and give horrified stares whenever you scrape your fork against your plate. Neither idea is fair.

This isn't true of *all* older women—or even of many. Scripture describes *godly* older women as having extremely valuable qualities: "Older women likewise are to be reverent in behavior, *not* slanderers or slaves to much wine. They are to teach what is good, and so train the young women" (Titus 2:3–4).

Yes, "young women" means us.

Here's a question: How does a girl who has rarely cooked anything beyond macaroni and cheese learn to be a keeper at home? How does a young mother lacking in wisdom become a Proverbs 31 woman? The answer is simple: Learn from the best. There are godly role models living and breathing at this moment who are eager to pass on their wisdom to the next generation. These godly older women were once less-godly, younger women who faced the same road that now stretches before us. They too have experienced challenges that tested their faith and called them to grow. And these same women are commanded to pass down the lessons they have learned to us. All we have to do is listen.

Although many times I've cried to my mom, "I don't have any good friends," I didn't realize what a precious gift I had. I wasn't friendless. I had *her*.

Many of us complain about not having true friends, but I think this is often because our eyes are not opened to the friendship possibilities around us. The world contains countless mothers and grandmothers who would cherish time spent pouring time and wisdom into our lives. (If you find any wisdom in this book, much of it will have stemmed from the inspirational lives and conversations from the Christian ladies I have known. I am indebted to them more than words can say.)

I cannot think of a single young woman in my acquaintance who does not have access to some kind of godly older woman. "Older" does not *necessarily* mean "senior citizen," but someone who has lived long enough that they have a mature outlook on life and insight to share. To a young girl, a woman in her twenties or thirties who has her head screwed on straight may qualify as a "godly older woman."

Generally, a girl's mom is her best mentor, but if you do not have a mother close by or if your mom is not a Christian, it may be wise for you to seek out a friendship with a woman at your local church who meets the Titus 2:3–4 qualifications.

BROTHERLY LOVE. LITERALLY.

Anyone who has ever possessed a dear, Christ-honoring friend can testify to the good they do. But sadly, we sometimes lose and overlook some other dear companions: the friends within our own family.

No friends care about me more than my family members. Unlike other just-barely-there-friends who pop in and out of my life, my family is stuck with me—for life. I'm unavoidable. If I'm depressed or having spiritual problems, they are the first to pick up on it; living in the same house, they naturally suffer the consequences.

While complete with faults and notable personality differences, our family members have been chosen. God chose them for us and us for them. He often chooses to place the packrat brother in the house of the obsessively organized sister so that they can both expand their horizons. The combination is supposed to better us both!

When I'm troubled in spirit, my parents give me wise counsel and pray diligently for me. Concerned for my best interests, they can bring to attention faults in behavior that I might have overlooked. Unmotivated by ulterior motives, they sincerely desire the best for me. And I can trust them.

If you've been given the enormous blessing of a Christian family, don't ignore them. They really are friend material.

Now, if you come from an abusive background or from a family that isn't concerned with following Jesus—please don't let this discourage you completely. I've really written these paragraphs for those who have Christian families but may be taking them for granted.

If you don't have a Christian family, you're not alone in that struggle. You don't need me to tell you that it's not easy—you know that well. But I really hope you'll take the initiative to plug in with a church family. Find a church that preaches the gospel and ask them to adopt you. Find older women at the church who are godly and ask if you can spend some time with them. Even if you don't have friends or a family God has connected you with by blood, you shouldn't have to live without Jesus-loving friends who are your family in spirit.

TITUS 2 MENTORING

Rethinking the purpose of friendship brings to light the fact that older women aren't such preposterous friends after all. Immense value can be found in the wisdom they impart. By spending time with godly older women—especially my mother, who is the primary female mentor God has given me—I can benefit from the wisdom they have gained through the years. Older women can keep me accountable in my actions and ensure that I remain a good model to others. Through them, the legacy of biblical womanhood can be passed on to light my generation. Maybe I'll even light the next.

I dwell in possibility.

—EMILY DICKINSON, poet

We hear about every other kind of women—beautiful women, smart women, sophisticated women, career women, talented women, divorced women. But so seldom do we hear of a godly woman—or of a godly man either, for that matter. . . . It is a much nobler thing to be a good wife than to be Miss America. . . . It is a far, far better thing in the realms of morals to be old-fashioned than to be ultra-modern. The world has enough women who know how to hold their cocktails, who have lost all their illusions and their faith. . . . The world has enough women who know how to be brilliant. It needs some who will be brave. The world has enough women who are popular. It needs more who are pure. We need women, and men, too, who would rather be morally right than socially correct.

—PETER MARSHALL, late chaplain of the United States Senate, *Mr. Jones, Meet the Master*

CHAPTER II

Ignition

Imagine what it would look like for a person to be completely sold out to the Cause. Imagine her heart, soul, mind, and strength consumed with knowing Him. Imagine how much joy it must bring to Christ when the people He shed His blood for live their lives out of love for Him.

Imagine the effect that one person could have.

I have an idea. It's not new or inventive, and it's only slightly radical, but I don't want to ever forget it. Instead of just complaining about the problems of the "beauty standards" and entertainment industry, let's reject them. Let's not allow those ideals to determine what we value. Instead of looking to celebrities, fashion magazines, movies, music, media, cliques, and peers to define ourselves, let's look somewhere else for that definition.

Are you sick of watching the women and girls around you hurting for truth? Do something about it. Help change their minds.

We've all heard the famous quote from Gandhi,

who encouraged people to "be the change you want to see in the world." The guy had a point. There comes a time when we should cease to criticize the problematic mind-sets around us and instead work proactively against them. Living out the gospel, for instance, means more than joining the "1,000,000 REAL Christians on Facebook" group. First, it means to live out what you believe.

Of course, it's easy to doubt that what we do carries weight. We secretly believe we are powerless, that our actions mean nothing. You might be thinking, "Hannah! Be realistic!" But I *am* being realistic.

Consider the power of the individual in this scenario.

LIKE A VIRUS . . .

As if a virus were sweeping over the entire earth, each country fell to its knees. The United States was the first to go. Its citizens began walking around with electronic devices planted in their ears. They began to withdraw from society, looking to these devices alone for companionship. From Barcelona to Tokyo, within a matter of weeks, not a single man, woman, or child in any developed country remained untouched. The world was taken over.

No, I'm not talking about the rise of World War III or the coming of the antichrist. I'm referring to something that has already happened.

I'm talking about the iPod.

How did the iPod become popular? A bunch of people

loved the idea, jumped on the new technology, and their friends began to take notice. Then their friends bought iPods, and their friends' friends bought iPods—and you get the picture.

Nearly every day, new messages, products, or ideas begin to gain popularity. Little-known books rise to the bestseller list. Random articles of clothing suddenly become popular. (Remember toesocks?) A small-town musician, whose fan base once consisted of his mother and Great-aunt Velma, gets a million viewers on YouTube.

How does this happen? The same way iPods became a fad—through individuals who cared enough to live out their enthusiasm. People spread messages. Not only celebrities or "important" people, but real, down-to-earth human beings can change the world with their level of enthusiastic living. You can, too.

IN CASE YOU'RE STILL SKEPTICAL

In looking back at history, we all recognize the bloodbath of the French Revolution. Untold numbers of innocent people were dragged to the guillotine during that dark time in history. What fewer people realize that at the same time as the French Revolution, England was on the verge of revolution, too.

Also sick and tired of corrupt government officials, England might've ended up like France if it had not been for two men: George Whitefield and John Wesley. As traveling preachers, riding on horseback throughout the English countryside, the men preached everywhere. "Everywhere" included bustling street corners, where the preachers were occasionally attacked by their audiences—who threw stones and chased the preachers through the streets.

They weren't popular or particularly cool people, but God used Whitefield's and Wesley's message—the gospel— to transform their troubled country dramatically. No longer did the English people look at their government as the source of human problems. Instead, they looked at themselves and questioned the sin in their own hearts. A bloody revolution was prevented because of the actions of two men.

So were these preachers full of witty comments and comedic timing? Um, not really. Overall, Whitefield and Wesley were pretty normal guys. Cut them and they would bleed red like the rest of us. Wesley had his share of weaknesses; he battled depression for much of his life and had marital problems. Whitefield wasn't particularly remarkable either; in fact, he was cross-eyed.

Neither was what we might call expert salesman material. Yet God used them in a powerful way, in spite of themselves. The story of Whitefield and Wesley shows how messages of immense influence can be passed through weak, feeble individuals. God wasn't bound by their personal inadequacies.

If God can used flawed, inadequate Christians, it means you and I can be used as well. We can make a very real dif-

ference with our choices. Nobodies like me can end up
kicking society into the gutter or cleaning up the streets.
People (like you) carry power, for bad or for good.

If you think about it, everyone is a trendsetter in her
own way, because everyone has an audience. Whether it's
a stadium full of people or just an observant little sister, we
each have some person or group of people who may be
influenced, consciously or subconsciously, by our example.

John Donne was on the right track when he wrote,
"No man is an island, entire of itself. Each is a piece of the
continent, a part of the main. If a clod be washed away by
the sea, Europe is the less."[1] At the time, Donne was musing
about death, about how each death diminishes humanity
as a whole, but the principle applies to the living, too.
While it's easy to leave the job of role modeling to those
with magnetic personalities—no man is an island. We are
connected to one another. Every foot, big or small, leaves
a print for others to follow.

Whenever I doubt whether my actions mean much
to others, Matthew 5:14 reminds me of the truth: "You are
the light of the world. A city set on a hill cannot be hidden."
No one within miles can miss the city lights of San Fran-
cisco or New York City. No matter if you think your example is significant, your actions "cannot be hidden." The
word used in the verse is definite. "Cannot" doesn't leave
much room for wondering, does it?

WHAT I'M NOT SAYING

So what exactly am I suggesting? I'm not saying that we can fix the world. I'm not asking for you to market my book, either. What I *am* saying is this: After you spend time reading about Christ, our sin, and how much it cost Him, at some point that information and your belief in it must translate into action. If we truly care about true beauty, purity, modesty, femininity, loving other people—and what we believe is true—then we can't sit still.

Now, what I once thought was extreme, I see as normal. What changed? Jesus changed me.

Enough complaints have been made about the problems, and we've discussed our beliefs at length. We know the solution to *all* problems is found in Christ. If a girl struggles with bulimia—God is there. If a girl wonders about purity—God is there, too. If any person is filled with sin (and we all are), that person desperately needs God's redeeming love—whether she knows it or not. Now what? What do we do with knowledge?

Now's the time to put the solution on banners and run through the streets like raving lunatics on a mission.

Don't let any fears get in the way between you and crazy, passionate worship. Forget about looking civilized. Forget about what others may think. With hoarse throats, exhausted lungs, and full hearts, let's proclaim the glorious loveliness of Jesus Christ as if we mean it. If we're genuinely passionate for His Cause, why shouldn't we?

I used to think such public expression was weird or radical. I used to want to hide myself in my bubble of Christian friends and never brush up against the world. That was then. Now, what I once thought was extreme, I see as normal. What changed? Jesus changed me.

The more I see who Jesus is, the more I glimpse the wise womanhood He's called us to, the more I see how the whole story of history revolves around Him—the more I realize how ridiculous it is to allow any inch of my life to escape His dominion. Every Jesus-follower is expected to . . . follow Jesus! I'm not talking about worship that kneels facedown 24/7, but worship in action.

You and I were called to be the dearly beloved of His soul (John 17:26; 1 John 2:4; 3:16–18). The nature of God's love is passionate, consuming. If we remain unchanged by it, we probably never encountered it in the first place.

Now's the time to step out of our way to pray with that anxious friend, encourage the classmate suffering from depression, be a friend to the junior-higher next door. So maybe those efforts do not exactly equate to running with banners, but taking initial steps *is* being faithful to Christ in small things, in actions that speak louder than any running-through-the-streets-screaming. We're saying, "I love You, too" to Christ through our lives.

And whatever Love motivates us to reach out in these ways—that must be a Love worth living for. That Love is what we're communicating.

OUR POWER AND RESPONSIBILITY

If we are going to recognize the power we have to affect other people around us, we also need to understand the *responsibility* we carry.

First Timothy 4:12 is often quoted to prove that "youth matter" to the church: "Let no one despise you for your youth, but set the believers an example in speech, in conduct, in love, in faith, in purity." It's pleasant to consider how much influence our actions carry, but I confess sometimes I squirm at the command to "set the believers an example." It's fun feeling important, but I just don't like being responsible for the consequences.

To quote that brilliant philosopher, the uncle of Peter Parker (otherwise known as Spiderman), "With great power comes great responsibility."[2] We can reach out to others, spread truth, and encourage the lives around us. This means we have great power. And along with that great power, we are also given the great responsibility to use it wisely.

Like it or not, we are trendsetters. Just as every fashion model ever to strut the runway, *we* affect the minds of others by what we wear. With such power, it's vital to question ourselves: *Am I an example of Christ-centeredness? Or have I just gotten comfortable in the "Christian routine" and forgotten why I've chosen to live this way?*

BUILDING WITH RIBBONS AND STICKS

What will be the grand result of our actions? Will we, like the iPod, take the world by storm? Will our influence set an example for others that will change the course of their lives? Will we reform the world?

Change happens when we choose to put Christ on the throne of *our* lives, tossing out all that stands in the way of His being total Master of our hearts.

I'm not claiming that we will. We know the world will never be perfect; it will be broken until Jesus returns to make it new. But as God-given "lights" in the world, I think our chances for change are better than we think (Matthew 5:14).

When I was about seven years old, my friend Marie and I developed the brilliant plan of building a fort in our backyard. While Mom didn't say no, she *did* caution us against placing our hopes too high. It was unrealistic that two little girls could build a fort (one that was safe, at least).

As if the odds against us weren't immense enough, Marie and I were *also* banned from using hammers and nails without adult supervision. A bit desperate, we finally found the materials for our fort: sticks from around the yard and ribbon. (Yes, the green, shiny kind used for wrapping up Christmas presents).

Did Marie and I succeed? With pathetic resources and even less experience, our prospects were dim, but the end results weren't too shabby. Our finished product was a shelter that could fit two small people (in a crouching position).

If one person comes to see more clearly the beauty and glory of Christ, that's a job well done.

While it wasn't exactly Fort Knox, the "fort" lasted two years until my dad eventually tore it down so he could mow the grass growing inside it. (If you're still not impressed, remember that we built the fort with *ribbons.*

And it lasted *two years*. I'm still a little proud.)

Many current endeavors could easily be compared to my fort. Looking at how huge the world is and how many voices are speaking to our friends and offering up different "truths," we may find it difficult to believe we can reach them. Hey, considering the different voices *we're* hearing, it's hard to believe sometimes that Jesus will ever be able to form us into His image or turn us into beacons of His grace.

But if we think instead in terms of the individual, the possibility makes more sense. Jesus isn't calling us to change whole cultures. He's calling us to seek Him *ourselves* and to reach out to our friends in His name.

So if you look at the challenge that way, change doesn't start on a large scale. It starts with renewing *our* minds daily in Scripture. Change happens when we help *our* little brothers and sisters understand the gospel. Change happens when we choose to put Christ on the throne of *our* lives, tossing out all that stands in the way of His being total Master of our hearts.

"Changing the world" really means changing the world for *individuals*. We are called to love people, plain and simple. If one person comes to see more clearly the beauty and glory of Christ, that's a job well done.

What is the challenge exactly? As I said before, it is almost embarrassingly simple: to change the mind-sets and hearts of those around us, by first changing ourselves. While it's easy to read and write about inner beauty, the challenge is to apply this to real life, and that's much, much harder.

Take comfort, though, because the change doesn't actually come from me and you. We're not working by ourselves. God is the initiator of everything, and there's no possible way to be faithful to this challenge without His constant grace (Ephesians 3:20). I like what Gary Haugen, a modern-day hero who works to set slaves free throughout the world, once wrote about the Cause:

There are those moments when we sense the call to goodness. . . . Indeed, it is the very reason for the journey and for our very being. *We were created for good works, prepared beforehand* . . . But drawing near the field, the clouds seem dark and the shadows long, and the challenge enormous. We doubt the joy and fear the risks. But wanting the good thing done, we ask, "Where is God?" We may even turn to Him and say, "You do it!" And lovingly our Father turns and beckons. "Come, I'll give you a boost in the saddle. We shall ride together." . . . We have a ride, with work and glory before us—a worthy struggle to engage alongside our Lord. A struggle for which we were made.[3]

THE ULTIMATE FACTOR

Above the opposition, the popularity of the role model, or the content of the message, there is a factor that ultimately decides a message's success. For instance, there must have been some invisible factor that caused iPod sales to break records. Was it a Mafia gangster in the back room of some seedy establishment, smoking a Cuban cigar and manipulating the markets to star Apple's music player? Was Steve Jobs using mind control to make Americans buy his product?

Hardly.

Jeremiah declared in Lamentations 3:37–38, "Who has spoken and it came to pass, unless the Lord has commanded it? Is it not from the mouth of the Most High that good and bad come?" And take a look at Proverbs 16:33: "The lot is cast into the lap, but its every decision is from the Lord." People can gamble with ad campaigns, but God is the ultimate factor. He decides which trends live or die.

We can't control results. Our job is obedience. But with God's help, our measly little actions can help bring about change—a transformation that begins with people who care so much about building forts that they'll use whatever they have, even if it's only ribbons and a pile of sticks, to get the job done.

The challenge is not to change the world (though I'm not going to complain if that happens to be the result!). The challenge is to act in obedience to the Savior, spreading the amazing truth He has entrusted to us, each and every day of our lives.

Who's with me?

And he who was seated on the throne said, "Behold, I am making all things new."
—REVELATION 21:5

It was when I was happiest that I longed most . . . The sweetest thing in all my life has been the longing . . . to find the place where all the beauty came from.
—C. S. LEWIS, *Till We Have Faces*

CHAPTER 12

Only His

I don't always feel passionate, it's true. And
then, sometimes, I feel passionate about stupid stuff. I
don't know about you, but I can get awfully worked up
over matters of opinion that really won't matter in a
year (or even in a month).

Then there are moments that are completely different. There are times when God seems to step down
from heaven just to give my shoulders a good shake.
There are times when I look at the stars and the sight
breaks my heart. I see my little sisters growing up, and
it makes me wish time didn't move so fast, and I long
for eternity. I read an old journal entry and end up in
tears because I'm not the same person I was before
and I'm so grateful for the changes.

You might have some similar memories.

So far, my life has been like one giant string, con-
necting those moments together. They're the only seconds that have truly mattered—when, unexpectedly,
I've stumbled over God. I see beauty that points me to
Him. I see brokenness that points me to how much we

need Him. I see how death is unnatural, and Jesus died to offer us life. I'm drawn into worship.

We cling to Him as He changes us; He doesn't ever let us go.

Whether it's been searching for Him or discovering that He's claimed me as His own, the sweetest part of my life has always been His.

I wish I would always remember that, that sin would never look attractive, because Jesus would be always on my mind. I wish I'd never chase another foolish cause again. I wish it were that easy. But, like the rest of the world, I am too "bent" to surrender easily to Him. Foolishness is too engraved into the human identity.

But all hope is not lost for you and me. While we must often find ourselves fighting to keep Him as our Cause, He fights for us. God promises to discipline those whom He loves, to push away our love for lesser things, and isn't that something we understand? We all know that if you love something, you fight to defend it. If it's in danger, you fight to save it. You don't let go easily.

We learned that from Him.

The pattern is simple. We cling to Him as He changes us; He doesn't ever let us go.

I have hope, too, for the day when Christ won't have to fight anymore. Of all the billions of angels in heaven, each face will be turned toward the face of Jesus. They'll want to see the look in His face when He sees me—when He sees each of us. (It's that way in weddings; if you want to see joy, just look at the groom's face.)

Jesus will be happy when He sees me. If for the joy set before Him, He endured the Cross, can you imagine what'll happen when He finally gets ahold of that joy? When He finally gets to grab us and never let go of our hands?

You are His joy. We're the lives Christ died to save. I can't begin to imagine what kind of climax and screaming hallelujahs we're going to hear in heaven when we meet Him.

One day Jesus is going to gaze on me with satisfaction. When He does, every bit of struggle, of fighting for Him to be my Cause, is going to be worth it.

"She's perfect," an angel might whisper, while the rest all say, "Hush!" Of course, we *will* be perfect, but only because His blood has washed our imperfections away.

You might think I'm overimagining that day. I'm frustrated because I know I haven't imagined it nearly enough.

I can't begin to imagine the glory that will be on display, the fear of God, the holiness, the love—here, this side of heaven, we lose all words.

Right now, from the cheap seats, our view of heaven is limited. We have no way of knowing what will transpire or even what's transpiring over our heads right now. We can't see with our own eyes how much God treasures us. We can't see His sovereign plan. We can't see much, really, at all.

All we know is that our inner transformation will be a long time in the making; we're not going to be perfect today or perfect tomorrow (unless God beams us to heaven today or tomorrow).

But this I know: One day Jesus is going to gaze on me with satisfaction. When He does, every bit of struggle, of fighting for Him to be my Cause, is going to be worth it. All the hours spent walking through heartache and searching for His face will dissolve into nothing but a memory of His faithfulness.

Examining you on that day, God won't find the same old self He's battled to protect and nurture throughout the years. The sin you once cherished will be harbored no more. He'll see His name etched across every vein of your heart.

And the sight will be beautiful.

HOW DO I KNOW IF I'M READY FOR MARRIAGE?

It's a question we'll all face, sooner or later. How do we find an answer? I suggest asking yourself these five not-so-simple questions:

1. "Am I of the legal age to marry?"

This is important! If you don't pass this question, don't worry about answering the rest of them yet!

2. "Am I mature enough emotionally for marriage?"

A few further questions might help you analyze your own emotional maturity. Are you constantly at odds with your family members? Do you find it difficult to overlook the shortcomings of others? Or are you able to live peacefully alongside those around you? After a conflict with a friend or family member, are you willing to accept blame?

3. "Am I responsible enough to be in a married relationship?"

In other words, are you faithful to complete the tasks you already have at hand? Do you spend your day responsibly?

4. "Would I be willing to submit to my future husband as the Bible commands?"

A good test for this would be whether you're currently living in submission to your parents.

5. "Would pursuing marriage better serve the kingdom of God than my remaining single?"

This one is the real humdinger!

If you answered all five questions with a yes, don't start jumping for joy yet. Now's the time to ask your godly mentors—that is, your parents and your closest, wisest, most gut-wrenchingly honest friends—to answer these same questions about you. The last question may especially require wisdom from God, so be sure to pray when thoughtfully considering your situation.

IS DATING OKAY?

A plethora of meanings exist for "dating" and "courtship." To some, "courtship" means going to a restaurant one-on-one and spending time together. To others, that's the same definition as "dating." What's the right path for twenty-first-century Christians?

Really, the important issue isn't "dating" vs. "courtship"; the terms mean very little. What *is* essential is whether purity is being pursued in the relationship. A guy and girl can technically be "courting" but know each other's bodies so well they might as well be married, whereas a "dating" couple can be wisely preparing for marriage in purity.

God doesn't use the words "dating" and "courtship" in the Bible, maybe because He knows how we tend to redefine those particular words to suit what we want. Instead, God presented principles for us to follow. Whatever the terms used, the necessary decision is whether God's principles will be obeyed. Here are purity principles from Scripture.

I. Guard your emotions and your body.

2. Avoid temptation like the plague. (Remember Joseph's story from Genesis?)

3. Be wise. (That is, don't trust your hormones. See Proverbs 7 . . . or pretty much the entire book of Proverbs.)

When nonbelieving guys and girls date for a few weeks, try each other on for size, and then move on to someone else, usually their idea is to nix all of the above principles. This is the world's dating model. Needless to say, pursuing romance without wisdom is unbiblical.

What is there to be done? If "dating around" is out, then what should marriageable Christian young people do?

Keep in mind that while biblical principles are unchanging, they do sometimes take different forms in different situations. For instance, a guy and girl who live next door to one another may have to set up different boundaries and get to know each other in a different manner than, say, a couple separated by a thousand miles who "date" mostly via phone and email.

Prayerfully search the Scriptures and discuss with godly mentors what the biblical standard for pursuing marriage and purity looks like. Seek guidance from wise married friends, books on the subject, your pastor, etc. And don't get anxious. God will be faithful to provide the answer at the right time.

HOW WILL I MEET THE RIGHT GUY?

As recorded in the book of Genesis, Abraham sent an employee to spy out a potential wife for his unmarried son. From the first, the employee balked. How was he supposed to successfully pick out a wife for *somebody else?* Abraham replied in perfect confidence, "The God of heaven will send his angel before you" (Genesis 24).

A wave of nausea probably swept through the employee's stomach as he began his search in Abraham's hometown. Centuries before "dating compatibility" and personality tests, the man was intimidated by the prospect of tracking down a prospective wife for the boss's son. He prayed that God would provide the right person for Abraham's son—and before the prayer was finished, a pretty, God-fearing girl named Rebecca asked if she could get him a drink of water.

The fact that Rebecca showed up at that very second

and inadvertently revealed her sweet, selfless heart in her simple offer to serve was quite . . . coincidental. But was it really coincidence? Abraham's servant obviously didn't think so. He considered it *providential.*

We know Rebecca's love story was divinely orches- trated by the God who leaves nothing to chance. Already He had molded Rebecca's heart so she possessed a rare sort of trust and courage that she would need. After all, she had to have the boldness to accompany this employee back to a foreign land and marry Abraham's son. For Rebecca, the proper time had come. She was ready.

So the point of this story is to promote arranged mar- riages—but not the type planned by human beings. God is the ultimate matchmaker. Like Rebecca's, our role is simply to nurture our faith and leave our futures to God. As Isaiah declared to an Israel that wondered if God was really concerned with their problems,

> Have you not known? Have you not heard? The Lord is the everlasting God, the Creator of the ends of the earth. He does not faint or grow weary; his under- standing is unsearchable. (Isaiah 40:28)

So you ask, "How will I meet the right guy?" The answer is, "God will introduce you." If you're supposed to get married, you *will.*

Waiting for God to "show up" and move us to that point is tough, but God never puts His children through situations that will not end in bringing glory to His name or nurturing His children in some vital way. He doesn't allow us to experience pain needlessly. Although we may never see the reason for the uncertainty, God has His reasons for making us wait. And it is the same God who divinely paired Rebecca and Isaac who asks us to trust Him.

MODESTY CHECKLIST

To be perfectly honest, I hate lists. They can be helpful for summarizing, but at the same time, they can completely distract from, say, the purpose of modesty.[1] All too often, people make up lists to replace the need to listen for the Holy Spirit. Rather than consulting God or conscience, we feel that if we live according to self-made criteria, God will be pleased with our obedience.

The danger is that we will start clinging to lists for our righteousness, rather than the grace Christ extends to us through the Cross. We can begin to look down on other people for not obeying our criteria and think that rules of our own invention make us extragodly. Lists can be dangerous because they can lead to legalism.

However, lists can also help connect abstract ideas to practical, day-to-day life. After some deliberation, I've decided to include my personal "Modesty Checklist" in this book. I'm not including it so you'll follow it to the letter or because I militantly believe people should follow *my* standards.

Instead I include this information to help get you thinking and praying about your own clothing. Since I didn't pull these points out of the sky (they've been gleaned from personal experience and advice from guys), I often use this list to help me be sensitive to the weaknesses of the guys around me. Again, there are no hard and fast rules—

just bullet points to get you thinking.

Make sure your heart first desires to please God. Real modesty doesn't exist until we submit ourselves to God's authority and desire to honor Him above our own preferences.

◆ Check your blouse or shirt. When you glance at yourself in the mirror, where do your eyes automatically travel—to your face or your chest? If your shirt accentuates or draws your eyes to your chest, that is where it will also draw the eyes of others.

◆ Bend down and touch the floor. Is your back still completely covered? If so, great! Generally, if a shirt extends two inches or more beyond your waistline when you are standing in a normal, nonslouching position, it will cover you when you bend over.

◆ Is what you are wearing transparent, tight, too short, lacking sleeves, or revealing any cleavage? Check your neckline. If a taller person were to stand next to you, is your neckline so loose that that person could see down your shirt? If so, wear an undershirt. If the undershirt does not succeed in covering you, then ditch the shirt and wear something else!

◆ Is the seat of your jeans or pants decorated with eye-catching embroidery, sequins, or words? These will automatically attract the eyes of those who see you from behind straight to your rear. Wearing these pants is probably not a great idea.

◆ Take a look at your skirt or shorts. Can you see higher than two inches above the knee while in a kneeling position? If your skirt has a slit, is it higher than two inches above your knee? If so, there is probably not much hope for it.

◆ It's a fact: Women do not see life through the eyes of men. We can look at an outfit and think, "Cute!" when a guy thinks, "Seductive." When there is a shirt or pair of pants you're not sure is modest, ask your dad or brother. If the item is questionable, consider not wearing it. Better to be safe than sorry.

Study Guide

Have you ever had a conversation with someone who really seemed to understand you? Your words made sense to that person, and when you lacked words to describe your feelings, he or she intuitively comprehended what you wanted to express. More than a conversation between two friends, it was the meeting of two souls. It was something special.

We like study guides, not because they're particularly interesting in and of themselves, but for the conversations they can spark. A study guide is useful for groups reading this book together because it can help direct the conversation to life-changing discussions.

If you're reading this book by yourself, don't turn away. We recommend picking out the study questions that are most thought-provoking for you and journaling your answers as you read. We pray this guide blesses you as much as writing it did us!

—HANNAH FARVER & LINDSEY WAGSTAFFE

CHAPTER ONE:
One Way to Get Sick

1. Have you ever felt insecure about your appearance? Have you ever considered yourself ugly?

2. How has the world's view of beauty affected you? Has it ever influenced your actions?

3. Do you feel concerned about the world's beauty standards and the cultural onslaught on women, especially young girls?

4. What do you think causes our culture to obsess over beauty?

5. Do you think our problems would be remedied if the world somehow did away with all magazines, billboards, and other material that show unrealistic beauty standards? Why or why not?

6. At what point does a desire to be accepted of and approved by others become wrong? How much should we let the opinions of others influence us?

7. Are insecurity, dissatisfaction with your appearance, and comparing your body with others' all serious issues, or do these only matter if you're actually harming yourself to "look better"? Why or why not?

8. Why do you think compliments and self-esteem-boosting techniques don't have lasting power to lift us up?

CHAPTER TWO:
On Love and Imitations

1. What words would you use to describe our culture's view of love?

2. Are there any people you've met or heard of who have demonstrated true love?

3. Are there people in your life who are difficult to love? What has loving them taught you?

4. The way many people talk about God's "love" for us, you'd think we must be pretty lovable—certainly nothing like Alexis or Gomer. Do you think this is true?

5. Look up Romans 5:8 and 1 John 4:9–10. Did Christ die for us because we were lovable people?

6. First Corinthians 13, the famous "love chapter," is usually read at weddings. In 1 John 4:8, it says that God is love. Have you ever read 1 Corinthians 13 as a description of God's love for you personally?

7. In the previous chapter, we discussed beauty. How do you think our pursuit for beauty is related to our longing for love?

8. What are some ways Christians tend to misuse and misunderstand the love of God? Do you think we talk about it enough in the church? Or do we talk about it too much—in the wrong way (in a way that makes God seem "tame and cuddly")?

9. Romans 5:5 says that the love of God is "shed abroad" in our hearts through the Holy Spirit (KJV). When was the last time you were utterly overwhelmed by the love of God and you felt it "poured out" on you, as some translations put it? Do you remember why?

10. How important is it for us to dwell on God's love on a daily basis, if we expect to grow in our Christian walk? Why? How does it affect and change us? Would you agree or disagree with the statement that "the love of God is the soul of the gospel"?

CHAPTER THREE:
A New Definition

1. Are you a Christian? If so, when did you repent and place your faith in Jesus Christ? What's your story?

2. Do you think Christians speak enough about "repentance"?

3. Do you ever find apathy in your own life? What do you do to fight it?

4. Have you ever met someone who was really and truly sold out to Christ? How was that person different from other people?

5. Are there any Christians (in history or currently living) whose life stories inspire you today? How did the knowledge of Christ's love set a pattern for them to love others?

If you don't know of inspiring Christ-followers, we recommend looking up Elisabeth Elliot, Amy Carmichael, Gladys Alyward, and/or Mary Slessor and learning about their amazing, God-centered lives.

CHAPTER FOUR:
The Beauty Cause

1. Read Psalm 139:13–14. The Hebrew word for "wonderfully" is *palah,* meaning "set apart" and "distinct." The Hebrew word for "skillfully woven" is *raqam,* meaning to weave together different colors. How is this significant in our view of beauty?

2. When we're in the habit of viewing our bodies through the world's eyes, our criticisms come automatically. The next time you look in the mirror and you're tempted to sigh, how can you start training yourself to think differently?

3. Even with the knowledge that God loves the way He made us, we tend to continue in our dissatisfaction with what He created. Why do you think this is? How can we counter this inclination?

4. If you think it may help you remember, print out Psalm 139:13–14 on an index card, and stick it on your bathroom mirror.

CHAPTER FIVE:
Deeper Than Skin

1. What does Hebrews 12:7–11 say about our struggles? Is God ever negligent of us? Does He care about our hearts?

2. Are there specific areas of your life that you see God working on recently?

3. Have you seen specific areas of your heart that have been changed by God throughout the years?

4. How much of your time is spent daily speaking to God? How much time each day do you spend talking to others?

5. Take a look at the quote from C. S. Lewis at the beginning of the chapter. What do you think it means? How does it apply to our spiritual selves?

CHAPTER SIX:
Beauty Killer

1. Have you ever considered how what you wear represents the gospel? Do you agree with the author's assertions on that subject?

2. Do you consider revealing, provocative clothing to be a demonstration of selfishness? Why or why not? Read Philippians 2:3–4. In your own words, what does this passage mean?

3. Do you think it is fair to refer to modesty as a "beauty killer"? Why or why not?

4. Do you often care what others think of the way you dress?

5. It's easy to rationalize our clothing choices when something looks really good on us. What are some of the excuses we usually come up with to suppress our consciences?

CHAPTER SEVEN:
Finding Femininity

1. Do you embrace the idea of femininity? Why or why not?

2. Do you think your perspective has been much shaped by feminism? In what ways?

3. What is your reaction to the word "submission"? Is it positive or negative?

4. Can you think of any specific ways you might serve your family?

5. What specific talents and/or interests do you have that you could cultivate to better serve your family?

6. How does biblical femininity translate into your life? How much does the Bible's opinion on gender roles affect your decisions/identity?

CHAPTER EIGHT:
'Cause You Need More Than a Guy

1. Do you ever struggle with keeping God the hope of your future, and not a future husband? If so, what practices have helped you to keep God first?

2. What are your tips and tricks for Bible study? Concordances? A Bible study curriculum? Coffee? Share your study secrets.

3. What are ways you can stay consistent in your personal Bible study?

4. Psalm 29:9 says, "The voice of the Lord twists the oaks and strips the forest bare" (NIV). Think about this in terms of the Bible as the Word of God. How should knowing this affect our attitude toward studying the Bible?

5. How often do you take time to think deeply about the cross, Christ's love, and all His death bought for you? Once a day? Once a week? Once a year?

CHAPTER NINE:
Purely Yours

1. Look up Romans 7:19–25. Are you serving God without distraction?

2. What do you think are possible distractions?

3. What can you do to eliminate the distractions?

4. What do you think about the concept of emotional purity? How is emotional impurity related to idolatry?

5. Titus 2:5 instructs young women to be "self-controlled" and "pure." How are the two related?

6. On our own, we're doomed to fail in the fight for purity. Read Titus 2:11–12. According to this passage, by what power can we live holy lives?

7. What kind of man would God desire you to marry, if marriage is His plan for you? Is it wise to make detailed, specific lists of nonessential requirements of what we want (or say that we "need") in a man? Why or why not?

8. Does your desire for a spouse rival your desire for God? Can God's love completely satisfy us? Does He?

CHAPTER TEN:
Another Love You Need

1. What are the qualities of a good friend? Look up and discuss Proverbs 27:17.

2. How many of your friendships would you define as "quality friendships"?

3. What are ways we work together with friends to glorify God? That is, how can we stir our friends toward Christ? How can we use our friendship for higher ends—making a difference and serving?

4. Do you have a friend who has stuck by you for a long time? What is it that has kept your friendship going?

5. What books, movies, and music influence you the most? Do you think the same criteria for defining "quality movies" or "quality books" hold true for measuring a "quality friend"?

6. Do you read books, watch movies, or listen to music that do not encourage your walk with Christ? Do you think this is wise?

7. Have you ever asked a friend to share their concerns for your spiritual life? If so, are you open to hearing their insights and possibly their rebuke?

8. Do you have a friend you can reach out to and encourage more effectively?

CHAPTER ELEVEN:
Ignition

1. Do you act out of obedience to Christ and a passion for His glory—or your own?

2. Do you set time aside every day for prayer and Bible study?

3. Do you try faithfully to obey God in public *and* at home?

4. Do you ask God for the grace to help you obey consistently?

5. What are *your* main spheres of influence?

6. What steps could you take to become a stronger influence of a Christlike attitude to friends, siblings, neighbors, relatives, etc.?

CHAPTER TWELVE:
Only His

1. Look up Psalm 37:27–29. What do these verses say about the character of God? What do they say about how we should live?

2. How do you spend your time?

3. Do you actively serve in your community?

4. When making decisions, do you consider how they affect others?

5. Do you really and truly look forward to heaven, the place where we will be united with Christ forever? If His presence was the only thing missing, would you still be satisfied there?

Acknowledgments

This will be a long list, since there were countless individuals God used to bless my life during the four years spent on-again-off-again working on this book. To those who critiqued, encouraged, or at least did not ignore me when I cried, "Help!" I thank you. Your words meant more than you know.

Mom and Dad, you're both amazing. It's impossible to count the blessings God's given through you, and I can't imagine my life without your guidance. Thanks for living what you believe.

To my brother, Tyler, and sisters, Grace and Miriam—you make me laugh way more often than any person deserves. I love and appreciate you so much.

Lindsey Wagstaffe, you once made me promise I'd write this in the acknowledgments: "I undistinguishedly, irrevocably, and unpathologically adore you, in spite of your unnaturalities."

Also Naomi Fleenen, you are a dear friend. I value your support, prayers, and friendship more than you realize.

There are many friends who supported this project with prayers, advice, criticisms, proofreading, volunteer hours at conferences, recommending it to friends, or by offering their input. Cy and Del Farver, Eunice Cowan, Sarah Betts, Gracy Howard, Olivia Snow, Kristin Braun, Hannah Lumpkin, Daria Woods, Hannah Fain, Kristin Personius, Christa and Kelly Taylor, Ashley Nicole Smith, Hannah Schlaudt, Lindsey Chance, Sydney and Rachel George, Ellen Lumpkin, Beth Chance, Stephanie Carrillo, Gabrielle and Michaella Elliott, David Boskovic/Jake Smith/Alex King (the fantabulous web designers/friends), Tim Sweetman, Alex Harris, Brett Harris, Carolyn McCulley and Mary Kassian (two wise women whose writings have helped me get a better understanding of strong, feminine womanhood), Christina Hastings, Charity Chambers, Katrina Martin, Paula Hendricks, and many others—I hope I can thank each of you in person soon.

Thank you, Kim Hendershot and Stacy Tardy, for gently pushing me to finish and reading through the early version.

The Village Church in Flower Mound, Texas—you've helped so much in my growth. I count you as a gift.

To the agents at Credo Communications who worked with me during the journey, David Sanford, Rebekah Clark, and particularly Karen Neumair for attentive reading and rereading during the manuscript's "final days"—you are so appreciated. (Thanks, Karen, for being such a sympathetic ear. I count you as both an agent and a friend—especially since you so kindly put up with my whining.)

Most of all, thank You, Jesus Christ. For life, for breath, for mercy. I feel like Bernard Clairvaux described himself, helpless to thank You enough: "Therefore what reward shall I give unto the Lord for all the benefits which He has done unto me? In the first creation He gave me myself; but in His new creation He gave me Himself, and by that gift restored to me the self that I had lost. Created first and then restored, I owe Him myself twice over in return for myself. But what have I to offer Him for the gift of Himself? Could I multiply myself a thousand-fold and then give Him all, what would that be in comparison with God?"

I love You, Lord.

Notes

The Truth about Causes (An Intro You Shouldn't Skip)

1. dc Talk, *Jesus Freaks Volume II: Stories of Revolutionaries Who Changed Their World*. Minneapolis: Bethany House, 2002. Accessed at www.jesusfreaks.net/excerpts/JF2_China.pdf.

Chapter One: One Way to Get Sick

1. South Carolina Department of Mental Health www.state.sc.us/##h /anorexia/statistics.htm © 2006.
2. Dr. Nancy Etcoff, Dr. Susie Orbach, Dr. Jennifer Scott, Heidi D'Agostino, "The Real Truth about Beauty: A Global Report." Commissioned by Dove, a Unilever Beauty Brand. 2004.
3. Medscape's *General Medicine* 6(3) 2004. (As cited by ANRED, www.anred.com/stats.html).
4. Centers for Disease Control, "Risk Behavior Surveillance," 2005, www.cdc.gov/mmwr/PDF/SS/SS5505.pdf.

Chapter Two: On Love and Imitations

1. "Love." *The American Heritage® Dictionary of the English Language, Fourth Edition*. Houghton Mifflin Company, 2004. Dictionary.com http://dictionary.reference.com/browse/love.

Chapter Three: A New Definition

1. Louie Giglio, as quoted here: http://firstimportance.org/2008/05/08 /god-in-skin-marching-steadily-to-the-beat-of-his-own-love/.
2. Paul Washer, message given 5/29/2006. www.sermonaudio.com/ playpdf.asp?ID=52906154239&sourceID=gcc.

3. Jonathan Edwards, "Sinners in the Hands of an Angry God," http://edwards.yale.edu/images/pdf/sinners.pdf. The Jonathan Edwards Center at Yale University, 2005.

4. KJV *Strong's References*.

5. Sam Storms, *One Thing: Developing a Passion for the Beauty of God* (Bathgate, Scotland: Christian Focus Publications, 2004), 19.

6. The paradox of grace and obedience, the meaning of legalism, and discipleship have taken me a long time to grasp. I'll be in heaven before I understand them fully; but if you want to delve deeper in these topics, I highly recommend reading C. J. Mahaney's *Living the Cross Centered Life* (Sisters, OR: Multnomah, 2006) and Tim Keller's *The Prodigal God* (New York: Penguin, 2008).

An Interjection

1. Dietrich Bonhoeffer, *The Cost of Discipleship* (New York: Touchstone, 1995), 44.

Chapter Four: The Beauty Cause

1. Sir Francis Galton, *Inquiries into Human Faculty and Its Development*, http://www.galton.org/books/human-faculty/ Copyright 1907.

2. "Miss Universe Composite," http://en.wikipedia.org/wiki/Image: Miss_Universe_manitou2121.jpg.

3. Gladys Aylward, as quoted by Elisabeth Elliot, *Let Me Be a Woman* (Carol Stream, IL: Tyndale, 1985), 32.

4. Bethany Patchin Torode, "The Eye of the Beholder," *Boundless* webzine. http://www.boundless.org/2000/features/a0000317.html.

Chapter Five: Deeper Than Skin

1. Actually, any cause—sex, money, friends, boyfriends, love—that pulls us from Christ, His glory, and His love needs to be replaced with what is truly worth the obsession!

2. John Piper, *Pierced by the Word* (Sisters, OR: Multnomah, 2003), 13.

3. Kris Lundgaard, *The Enemy Within* (Phillipsburg, NJ: P&R Publishing, 1998), 47.

Chapter Six: Beauty Killer

1. John Keats, "Endymion."

2. Webster's 1828 Dictionary.

3. Dannah Gresh, "The Clothes Crisis," *Christian Parenting Today.* www.christianitytoday.com/cpt/2002/005/4.44.html.

4. Shaunti Feldman and Lisa A. Rice, quoting an anonymous man, *For Young Women Only* (Sisters, OR: Multnomah, 2006), 103.

5. Patrick A. Means, *Men's Secret Wars* (Grand Rapids: Fleming H. Revell, 2001), 138–39.

6. The Rebelution's Modesty Survey. www.therebelution.com/mod estysurvey.

7. Mary Kassian, *Girls Gone Wise* (Chicago: Moody, 2010), 97–100, italics mine.

8. C. J. Mahaney, *Living The Cross-Centered Life* (Sisters, OR: Multnomah, 2006), 21.

9. To help you think through your wardrobe and make wise decisions about what to wear, see the Modesty Checklist at the back of this book.

Chapter Seven: Finding Femininity

1. I'm writing under the assumption that abortion and homosexuality are sins. (Divorce is sometimes sin, but not in every circumstance.) See 1 Corinthians 6:9–10, Romans 1:26–28, Mark 10:9, 1 Corinthians 7:10–11, Romans 8:1. These are each huge issues, and I don't want to paint with too broad a brushstroke. My main point is that *something* brought about society's acceptance of these behaviors. In the early part of the twentieth century, homosexuality was taboo, and abortion, although existent, was miles away from its current status. In the '60s, feminism helped create a culture where it was acceptable to challenge moral standards. It's no coincidence that abortion and homosexuality were let loose and soon after became "normal."

2. Ani DiFranco, www.brainyquote.com/quotes/authors/a/ani_ difranco.html.

3. Phyllis Trible, as quoted by Mary Kassian, *The Feminist Mistake* (Wheaton, IL: Crossway Books, 2005), 129.

4. Annie Laurie Gaylor, "Feminist Salvation," *The Humanist,* July/August 1988, 37, italics mine.

5. Jone Lewis, "Andrea Dworkin Quotes," http://womenshistory.about. com/od/quotes/a/andrea_dworkin.htm.

6. Sally Miller Gearhart, "The Future—If There Is One—Is Female," *Reweaving the Web of Life* (Gabriola Island,British Columbia: New Society Publishers, 1983).

7. Wayne Grudem and John Piper, *Recovering Biblical Manhood and Womanhood* (Wheaton, IL: Crossway Books, 2006), 38–39.

8. Alexis de Tocqueville, trans. Henry Reeve. *Democracy in America, Vol. 2* (London: Longmans, Green, 1875), 194.

9. Carolyn Mahaney, *Feminine Appeal* (Wheaton, IL: Crossway Books, 2004), 109.

10. For flawed, human, but worthwhile heroines, see Deborah, Abigail, Miriam, Ruth, Mary, or the women who characterize wisdom in the book of Proverbs. Or read up on the works and lives of Jane Grey, Elisabeth Elliot, Abigail Adams, Isobel Kuhn, Amy Carmichael and Joni Eareckson Tada.

Chapter Eight: 'Cause You Need More Than a Guy

1. Tim Keller, *Counterfeit Gods* (New York: Penguin Books, 2009), "Introduction," xvii.

2. A transcription from a pair of sessions given by Pastor Matt Chandler at the "Acts 29 Bootcamp," as quoted on this blog: http://cawley. typepad.com/blog/2005/04/defining_succes_3.html.

3. John Piper, "Is Jesus an Egomaniac?" message given at the Passion 2010 conference. http://www.beautyfromtheheart.org/2010/01/ is-jesus-egomaniac.html.

4. Joni Eareckson Tada and Steve Estes, *When God Weeps* (Grand Rapids: Zondervan, 2000), 127.

5. Kevin DeYoung and Ted Kluck, *Why We're Not Emergent: By Two Guys Who Should Be* (Chicago: Moody, 2007), 37.

6. From Jim Elliot's journal, as quoted by his wife, Elisabeth Elliot, *In the Shadow of the Almighty* (New York: HarperOne, 1989), 58.

7. "Work," Jars of Clay, *Good Monsters* (Essential Records, 2006).

8. Francis Schaeffer, *Letters of Francis A. Schaeffer* (Wheaton, IL: Crossway, 1985), 109.

9. C. J. Mahaney, *Living the Cross-Centered Life* (Sisters, OR: Multnomah, 2005), 41–42.

10. Elliot, *In the Shadow of the Almighty*, 58.

11. Charles H. Spurgeon, *Faith's Checkbook* (New Kensington, PA: Whitaker House, 1992), entry for June 22.

Chapter Nine: Purely Yours

1. L. E. Kastner, A *Glossary of Colloquial French Words* (1929, available on Universal Digital Library), 182.

2. Suzanne Hadley. "Seven Myths Single Women Believe," *Boundless* webzine, published April 5, 2007. http://www.boundless.org/2005/articles/a0001480.cfm.

3. Lindsey Wagstaffe, www.beautyfromtheheart.org.

4. Elisabeth Elliot, *Passion and Purity* (Grand Rapids: Revell, 2002), 40.

5. John Piper, *Pierced by the Word* (Wheaton, IL: Crossway, 2006).

6. Elliot, *Passion and Purity*, 72.

7. Josh McDowell, *The Secret of Loving*, as quoted in *Christianity Today*, November 12, 2001 http://www.christianitytoday.com/ct/2001/november12/25.94.html.

8. For information about or sermons on audio by Matt Chandler, check out www.thevillagechurch.net. This story is taken from the sermon "The Shepherd and His Unregenerate Sheep," given at the 2009 Desiring God pastors' conference. The full sermon is available at www.desiringgod.org.

Chapter Ten: Another Love You Need

1. This is the version of the story told by my friend Lindsey Wagstaffe. If Aesop never actually wrote this, please take it up with her.

2. Shane Claiborne, *The Irresistible Revolution* (Grand Rapids: Zondervan, 2006), 134–35.

3. Voddie Baucham, *The Ever Loving Truth* (Nashville: B&H Publishers, 2004), 36.

4. Lindsey Wagstaffe, "Judge Thy Neighbor?" http://www.beautyfromtheheart.org/2008/11/case-for-judgment.html.

Chapter Eleven: Ignition

1. John Donne, "No Man Is an Island."
2. *Spiderman*, Sony Pictures, 2002.
3. Gary Haugen, *Terrify No More* (Nashville: Thomas Nelson, 2010), 242–43, italics mine.

Modesty Checklist

1. See the quote from Mary Kassian in chapter 6, "Beauty Killer."

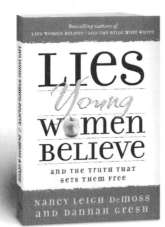

LIES YOUNG WOMEN BELIEVE

Lies Young Women Believe will give girls aged 13-19 the tools they need to identify where their lives and beliefs are off course—the result of buying into Satan's lies about God, guys, media, and more. It isn't enough to identify these lies, however. The authors are well-equipped to lead young women in the skills and the truths of Scripture that overcome those lies.

ISBN-13: 978-0-8024-7294-6

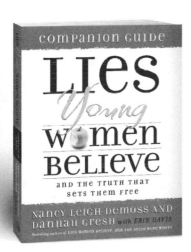

THE COMPANION GUIDE FOR LIES YOUNG WOMEN

Get the resource that helps you go deeper into the truths found in *Lies Young Women Believe*. The Companion Guide contains questions and activities that will cause readers to think and wrestle with the truth in their search for answers to life's tough questions.

ISBN-13: 978-0-8024-7291-5

MOODY
PUBLISHERS

moodypublishers.com